The Effective Board

The Effective Board

by **CYRIL O. HOULE**

Association Press
New York

Foreword

FROM Tocqueville in the 1830's to the most recent exchange student, discerning foreign observers have commented on the American capacity for voluntary association. Early generations of Americans associated themselves for mutual protection and mutual aid. Volunteer fire departments, corn-husking bees, and barn raisings demonstrated the values of co-operative effort; and lecture series, literary, and library societies developed as a response to the desire for self-improvement. At a later date, hospital dispensaries, orphanages, and relief societies were the responses to illness and poverty. Today American society is characterized by a bewildering variety of voluntary associations aimed at social improvement. The purposes range from the trivial to the profound. Their importance ranges from the negligible to the significant in impact. In their totality, they are responsible for a great part of the color, vigor, and strength of American society.

The capacity and desire to form a voluntary association is, however, no guarantee of effectiveness and usefulness. The effectiveness of an organization flows from the wisdom and clarity with which the board of directors performs its policy-making and leadership role. In order to make his maximum contribution, each board member should prepare himself for board membership. Intuitive skills need to be supplemented by reading, study, and careful observations. Happily, in some communities the efforts of the conscientious board member are supported by carefully organized board-member training institutes.

The University College of The University of Chicago and the Welfare Council of Metropolitan Chicago have shared a conviction about the significance of policy-making boards in guiding community services. These two organizations have also shared a concern for helping the conscientious board member to prepare himself for effective participation in board activity. Out of this concern came an annual board-member training institute co-sponsored by the University College and the Welfare Council.

During the past ten years the training institute has been exceedingly fortunate in the continuing leadership of Dr. Cyril O. Houle, Professor of Education of The University of Chicago. His insights into board process, his warmth, and his skill in adult education have combined to produce a continuously rewarding board-member training program. Those who have studied with him have not only enriched the life of the boards on which they serve but they have also gained greater personal satisfaction in the performance of a civic duty.

Dr. Houle has been persuaded to recast his teaching materials in book form and thus share the content of the training program with a wider audience. The reader will find helpful insights and practical suggestions in every chapter. The book is written with the clarity that comes from mastery of the subject matter. The experienced board member as well as the beginner will find help in these pages. It is also commended to agency executives. *The Effective Board* should increase the number of effective boards in American communities.

ROBERT H. MACRAE, Executive Director
Welfare Council of Metropolitan Chicago

Preface

THE knowledge, insight, and capacity required of a good board member are products of experience and of reflection about experience.

People learn to be on boards by being on boards. The person who learns to swim must do so in water; only there can he get the true feeling of the environment to which he must manage to adjust. Similarly only when one is immersed in the affairs of a board can one gain a full sense of its complex and interrelated pressures.

But a board is not necessarily good because it exists; it can be no better than its own members know how to make it. Because many boards are mediocre or incompetent, the learning they provide is poor or negative. "I have always noticed," observed General Goethals, "that a board is long, narrow, and wooden." Perhaps his remark was too sweeping, but it graphically describes an all-too-familiar phenomenon. The most such a board can offer is the opportunity to practice mistakes. Even when a board is good, it may conduct its affairs in such a way that a long time is required before new members become fully adjusted to their roles. Sometimes they sink before they learn to swim.

Fortunately the education required is never wholly a by-product of experience. Board members must constantly make judgments and discriminations. By doing so, they gradually achieve understanding and sophistication. Also they have many opportunities to learn from others—by direct discussion, by reading, or by attending special seminars and courses. Just as the swimmer profits from instruction, so may the board member.

All boards, however various their natures and purposes, have certain essential similarities. The study of good board practice can therefore greatly shorten the time board members need to learn how to be effective. The purpose of this book is to introduce them to such study.

A longer, more comprehensive, and more theoretical analysis of boards will be published later. It is my hope that many who read this book will send me their reactions to it and their suggestions for change. The additional experiences they describe in the effective operation of their own boards will enrich the future work.

Grateful acknowledgment is made to the Welfare Council of Metropolitan Chicago, to the Chicago Community Trust, and to University College of The

University of Chicago for the encouragement and support which facilitated the preparation of the manuscript; to Robert MacRae for writing the introduction; to Joan Moore and David Jickling who served as research assistants; to Ruth S. Moore of Community Programs Counselors for assembling the first draft; and to the following people who read this book in manuscript: Lawrence A. Allen, Mrs. Evelyn S. Byron, Roald F. Campbell, Francis S. Chase, Luvern L. Cunningham, Maurice F. X. Donohue, Miss Eleanor S. Ferguson, Mrs. Robert L. Foote, Earl Hargett, Mrs. John A. Holabird, Mrs. Cyril O. Houle, Meyer Kestnbaum, John I. Kirkpatrick, Mrs. Frank D. Mayer, Robert H. MacRae, Mrs. George A. Ranney, Jr., Mrs. Jack Vilas, Jr., and Anthony G. Weinlein. All of them tried to make the book better, but I alone am responsible for the final result.

Since it has taken a good many years of reading, experience, and discussion to develop these materials, I am keenly aware of the apparently endless variety of situations in which boards are found and the incredible complexity of the problems they confront. In this introductory volume, the principle of maximum utility must guide the selection of material. A chapter could easily be written on each of the sections of this book. Moreover, there are countless circumstances which are vital to some boards but are not common enough to permit treatment here. Some of the suggestions may seem obvious, but experience has taught me that they are sometimes not understood even by fairly sophisticated board members.

The contents of this book are based upon observations made by board members who learned their way by being on boards and evaluated their experiences while participating in an organized board training program. Annually for the past ten years, new and veteran board members have, by their discussion, helped to develop the principles and practices which are set down here. These experienced men and women provided the testing ground which related theory to practice. They raised the questions. They sharpened the answers. They applied the conclusions. They are the authors behind the lines of print on these pages.

The Effective Board is their book. It is dedicated to them on the tenth anniversary of the Board Members' Training Program.

—CYRIL O. HOULE

How to Use this Book

This book has been designed to serve both those who are interested in boards in general and those who would like to improve a specific board. In carrying out this latter function, it may be useful to rate the board according to the scale which will be found in the Appendix. Beginning in Chapter Two, certain sections of the book are numbered in bold face type in order to help relate each of them to the various principles included in the rating scale. On the last pages of the book the reader will find a key which links the desirable board characteristics to the appropriate numbered sections which discuss them.

Contents

(Chapter) (Page)

CHAPTER ONE

How to Think About a Board

Most of the affairs of American life are controlled or influenced by boards. In government, in business, and in the countless associations by which people seek to achieve common purposes, councils of citizens acting together exercise guidance and direction. The normal activities of life may not seem, on the surface, to be governed by a board but, when examined more closely, they very often reflect the fact that somewhere, around a conference table, a group of people have come together and made decisions.

Consider the ordinary citizen, living anywhere in the United States. If he works for a private corporation or for any of a number of public services, his conditions of employment and his chances for advancement are governed by a board. His children are educated in schools, colleges, and universities whose policies are controlled by boards. The church at which he worships, the organized efforts to improve society in which he plays a part, and the institutions

1

in which he seeks knowledge and enlightenment are usually guided by boards. If he belongs to a union or to a professional or trade association, the conditions of his membership and the services he receives will be influenced by a board. If he gives to charity, his money is spent by a board and, if he receives private charity, the terms under which he receives it are established by a board. If he is ill or if he needs other kinds of special care, he usually goes to an institution which is operated by a board. Many of the services of government which he supports with his taxes are directed by boards. Board influence is, in fact, so much a part of his life and environment that like the air he breathes, he scarcely knows that it is there.

To become properly aware of the true nature of familiar objects and influences, it is necessary to bring them squarely into view, examining them with the same wonder and curiosity with which one would inspect the rare or the previously unknown. When boards are subjected to this scrutiny, they are seen to be extraordinarily complex in their form and in their operation. Before it is possible to deal with one effectively, it is necessary to learn how to think about a board.

HOW BOARDS BEGAN

Boards were rare in pioneer days. The man who depended on his own initiative and skill to leave the settled East and move westward, to clear the land, to build his shelter, and to clothe and feed his family

2

was also a man who expected to have a direct voice in every decision which influenced his life. Even when the clustering of people made government necessary, everybody decided everything. The New England town meeting was a pure democracy. Each issue down to the location of the village pump or the selection of the schoolteacher was decided by a common vote after all arguments had been heard. The smaller the community, the hotter the debate.

As time went on, as cities grew, as life became longer and more complex, and the problems and institutions of common life multiplied, citizens could no longer directly control all aspects of their society. They created their city councils, their legislatures, and their Congress to deal with general matters. But since government often seemed remote and essentially negative in character, it was watched with a close and jealous regard. Some matters, it was felt, could not be safely left to the general authority of government. Therefore special boards began to develop, boards which had responsibility for schools, for health, for welfare, for libraries, for universities, for museums, or for homes for the handicapped.

In private affairs, also, growth has led to the delegation of responsibility. Clubs, unions, charitable groups, and other forms of voluntary association usually began with pure democracy. Everybody decided everything. But the ones which flourished and increased in size sooner or later abandoned direct control of all activities by all the people and vested au-

3

thority in the hands of a central group. The result was the creation of a board, or a group of people which was called by another name but was essentially a board. This process has taken place very often in the past and still continues to be important today.

But boards have also grown up in another way. Our society affords great opportunity to the individual citizen who sees a social need and dedicates himself to meeting it. It has been well said that every great social movement begins first as an idea in the mind of one person. But no one person can build and preserve an institution alone. This fact is particularly evident when the leader's strength begins to fail and his capacity and personality can no longer exert a powerful spell. Then those who were his advisers and helpers gradually take over responsibility, and organize to preserve the institution he created and to formalize his work. The shadow of the founder is lengthened by the creation of a board.

This kind of extension has been most notable in the development of private services, particularly in education, health, and welfare. The boards concerned with such functions usually have no large groups of people from whom they derive their authority. But, though they do not directly represent the community as its chosen delegates, they do represent the best qualities of the community—in vision, in service, and in responsibility.

The two processes of representative government and of institutionalization have been embedded so deeply in American life that the pattern of board control has been firmly set. When a new organization is formed or an old one extended to some new area of service, it is natural for a board to be created to provide the necessary control and support. If a YMCA is to be founded, for example, its sponsors will usually begin by creating a board. The same process now occurs so naturally and so universally that it is likely that most modern boards did not evolve from some other earlier institutional form. They came into existence at the same time as the service they control or the function they discharge.

THE BASIC NATURE OF THE BOARD

Though boards have grown up in various ways and in many situations, they have come to have a number of common characteristics.

To begin with, a board is always related to some institution or service or association—a school, a business, a settlement house, a church, a hospital, a service club, a Junior League, or some effort of a group of people to carry on a useful function. The over-all goal of the board is and must be the same as the goal of the agency or association with which it is connected. If the members of a board ever begin to think chiefly of other things—of their own prestige, of making a profit or helping their friends, or using the board to advance their private ends—they lose sight of their proper function and the result is unhappy.

The board's relationship to its institution or serv-

5

ice or association is one of both control and assistance. The board may have ultimate power or its authority may be sharply limited, but it always has some responsibility to make policies and see that they are carried out. The members of a board must also provide aid in furthering its work. For example, they may need to interpret the program to the community, they may need to raise money, and they may need to put their special talents or contacts to use. Unless a board accepts responsibility for both control and assistance, its proper functioning is impaired.

A board is made up of individuals, each with his particular personality, ideas, prejudices, and habits. Each has his own reasons for being on the board and his own idea of his relationship to it and to his fellow board members. To think of a board only as a group of people is to fail to understand it. To the outside world or to its own subordinates, a board sometimes appears to be an august assemblage, wrapped in mystery, and speaking with a clear and unanimous voice. Any meeting of any board shows how false that picture is.

And yet, in the strictest sense, the board is collective in its nature. So far as it is concerned, an individual member has no control over the work of the agency except when the board is in session or when he is performing some task that the board as a whole wishes to have performed. In effective board operation, individual personalities must be blended together into a functioning group which has its own spirit, tone, and quality. The board must be able to achieve consensus or to define a majority opinion which reflects the wishes of as many of its members as possible. They, in turn, must accept the obligation to work as a group. As Alfred North Whitehead once remarked, no member of a crew is praised for the rugged individuality of his rowing.

A board is always related in some way to the world outside both itself and the institution, service, or association it controls. If it is a public board, it must fit into the structure and politics of the unit of government of which it is a part. If it is a private board, its formal relationship to an outside public may be less clear-cut, but its informal network of contacts is usually very broad. Whether public or private, the board has a special duty to be sure that the program is understood and supported in whatever may be its own natural community.

Finally, a board must work with an executive and staff who have rights and responsibilities of their own. Sometimes the paid workers have only the authority granted by their terms of employment or won by their own personal qualities. In many cases, however, the executive and the staff have a special authority which arises out of their professionalism. In most cases the board selects them and removes them from office; their power derives from the power of the board. And yet the board is not dominant so far as the profession they represent is concerned. A school board, for example, may select a school superintendent but it must do so only from among the limited sphere of those who are judged by established standards to be competent educational administrators. In each kind of situation the relationship has its own distinctive character. The relation of a Protestant church board to its minister is not the same as that of a public library board to a librarian or a private hospital board to a hospital administrator. In all such cases, however, the essence of the relationship is the same: a lay, part-time, usually unpaid board controls the operations of a professional, full-time, paid executive and staff.

WHY BOARDS ARE IMPORTANT

The widespread existence of boards means that they possess values which are apparently essential to modern life. It will be useful therefore to assess the reasons why boards are so important.

The central value of the board is that it provides an opportunity for the use of collective wisdom. Ideally it places at the disposal of a program the knowledge, insight, and personal contacts of a group of people who are unusually able and who have widespread spheres of influence. Important consequences result. The right decision is more likely to be arrived at if several minds seek it together. In the weighing of alternatives, collective judgment is of crucial importance. The executive and staff have, in the board, a part of the whole community whom they can readily consult and who can give them confidence in the wisdom of their decisions. The citizen has a breadth of viewpoint which gives him a perspective on the work of the agency; he can keep it from becoming too specialized and narrow.

The board is also a powerful means of securing support in the general community if the special competence and contacts of particular board members can be used effectively. The board as a whole explains and interprets present activities and builds support for further advances in program. It provides liaison with other related enterprises. In no other way can there be built the base of confidence and support which a broadly related board can furnish.

Boards provide, too, for continuity of policy and program. Executives may come and executives may go, but the board goes on forever. It endures, though its membership changes, just as the human body remains essentially the same although the cells are constantly replaced.

Boards have a value for all society since they provide one of the most significant means for preserving the democratic spirit. The huge government bureau, the tremendous industry or union dominated by one man, or the impersonal social agency or association does not provide a sufficient flexibility to command the continuous and creative use of human intelligence. But when planning is spread throughout society, when it is not restricted to a few people at the top, when it is infinitely modulated to local conditions and local wishes, it becomes alive and vital.

9

Every citizen whose interests extend beyond himself and his home has a good chance of being on a board. For a time he takes his place as one of those who accept responsibility for making and carrying out decisions. He knows at first hand the experience of working with others in the joint effort to maintain and improve a program. He learns how policies are set and rules made. By the time he is succeeded by someone else who has been chosen by the same process that he was, he has come to understand the nature of democratic authority. He respects and supports it, for he has known and exercised it himself.

Participation causes a board member to grow in social stature and understanding. It is through board membership that a constant new supply of leaders is trained for our society. Those who are successful on one board are often asked to take on new and larger responsibilities with other boards. It is this process of the broad acceptance of authority, with citizens moving in and out of positions of responsibility, which helps to give meaning and tone to American society and trains the leaders who are needed for the improvement of the democratic life of this country. As a library trustee once observed, "I know I won't leave much money to my children, and certainly not a distinguished name, but I do think it is a sort of legacy for them that I should be the kind of person who is appointed on the library board."[1]

---

[1] Anna Gertrude Hall, *The Library Trustee* (Chicago: American Library Association, 1937), p. 137.

THE MAJOR TASK OF THE CHAIRMAN OF THE BOARD

The happy results suggested in the last section do not occur automatically. They can be won only by constant effort, and, because the board is essentially a group of people governing itself, this effort must be shared by all the members.

The primary task of the chairman of the board is that of helping diverse personalities merge into an effective social whole. In the operation of a board, the interaction of the personalities of the members is of the greatest significance. It is the chairman's task to lead and to restrain, to blend in proper proportion the more capable and vocal members with the less experienced and silent ones. It is his job to foster such a unity of purpose and such a loyalty to objectives that each individual realizes that his own judgment is a part of the collective wisdom of the board.

One point should be noted here, although it will be amplified later. It is the chairman's task to administer the board, and it is the executive's task to administer the program. Whenever the reverse happens, the worst possible trouble is almost certain to occur.

THE INFINITE VARIETY OF BOARDS

Boards are so numerous, so universal, and so intimately woven into the fabric of American life that they have developed almost every conceivable pattern and form. We shall not pause long at the task of

11

defining and categorizing them nor of illustrating all their infinite varieties, for such is not the purpose of this book. But later pages will be clearer if a few general observations are made at this point.

The definition of a board, then, as it is used in this book, is *an organized group of people collectively controlling and assisting an agency or association which is usually administered by a qualified executive and staff*. Three different kinds of boards may be identified.

The first is the *controlling board,* which usually possesses the immediate and direct legal responsibility for the work of an agency. (And here, at once, there is another word to define. The term *agency* is a bland one, whose very colorlessness permits it to be given a variety of meanings. It signifies here any organization or service which has been established to achieve a social purpose. This usage of the word comes from the field of social work, but the term will be used in this book to cover a variety of forms such as school systems, hospitals, universities, private child care agencies, libraries, and churches.) A controlling board—whether public or private—is usually responsible for the work of the agency, and the executive and staff are usually subordinate to such a board.

An *auxiliary board* is one which has been created (usually by the controlling board) to carry out certain agreed-upon responsibilities. For example, the women's board of a hospital may undertake to direct volunteer services, to raise money, and to promote

12

good public relations. In some cases, auxiliary boards develop an extensive life of their own, and they may have a great deal of prominence, but they are never in possession of the fundamental powers and responsibilities of the controlling board but only of such power as it delegates to them.

An *associational board* is the chief mechanism of continuing responsibility for a voluntary membership group, such as a club, a fraternal body, a professional society, a union, or a special interest league. The basic responsibility of the associational board is to its own membership, and the desire to express the common will of the members must always be its central guiding aim. Sometimes associational boards do not have an executive and staff to carry out the work of the program. Also it should be noted that some organizations which call themselves associations are really agencies.

The agencies and associations already mentioned in this chapter only illustrate the number of different kinds of programs and services which usually fall under the control of a board. Perhaps an additional list may indicate something of the range of the parts of society which come under board control. Such a list would include settlement houses, day care centers, services for the handicapped, and specialized health units; museums; foundations and other organizations to advance special interests such as international relations, racial and religious tolerance, and planned parenthood; commissions controlling special facili-

13

ties such as bridges, harbors, recreational areas or monuments; civil service commissions, licensing boards, penal authorities, and institutions; recreational authorities; and conservation agencies.

On the surface, the boards of corporations organized for profit might also seem to fall within the scope of the present treatment. Actually, however, such boards may be very different from other kinds of boards in the exercise of their power. They may, in fact, be nothing more than co-ordinating and planning committees made up of the central administrative officers of the company, with perhaps a few other persons added. Studies of corporation boards made by the Harvard School of Business tend to treat the central officers and the board of the company as a single social unit in which each individual may play several roles but in which there are no sharp structural distinctions among board, executive, and staff. Though these distinctions appear to be growing and the pattern in corporations is becoming more like that of other agencies, the ideas suggested in this book may be of only limited use to most corporation boards.

There are many other kinds of corporate bodies which also lie on the fringe of the board as it is defined here. To choose only a few examples, there are legislatures, judicial bodies, executive bodies, advisory bodies, standing committees, and fictitious boards called into being for no purpose other than to comply with legal requirements or to secure pub-

14

lic relations advantages. In such cases, the reader should judge for himself whether the suggestions made in this book are relevant.

MORE DEFINITIONS

In addition to the terms already defined, a few others should be made clear, chiefly because they are used in rather general ways to signify a large number of people or things which, in practice, are often given a variety of names.

The *executive* is the person who directs the actual operation of the agency or association under the general control of the board to which he is responsible. Usually he is a professional person and is paid for his services.

The *staff* refers to the people who are employed in an agency to carry out its work under the direction of the executive. As here used, the term does not include the executive himself.

The *program* refers to the total range of services or activities provided by the agency or association.

A *policy* is a settled course of action which is ordinarily based on the application of a principle or a group of principles. Policies are adopted by the board, although they are usually discussed with, and may be proposed by, the executive. Examples of policy decisions might be these: that of a welfare agency which decides to institute a schedule of charges for its services although they have previously been free; that of a school board which decides to develop a new

15

junior college; and that of a library board which decides to establish a salary schedule for its professional staff.

The *constituency* of an agency is that part of the general public which is particularly concerned with the work being undertaken. In public agencies, the constituency is made up of the citizens of the unit of government concerned. In private agencies, the constituency is often rather arbitrarily defined, being made up of stockholders, contributors, or those who have expressed an interest in the program. Many private agencies have no formal constituencies at all.

The *clientele* of any agency is made up of the people it serves.

Since the English language has no singular pronoun to refer to both sexes, it has been necessary in this book to adopt the customary practice and use the masculine form throughout in order to avoid the monotonous expression "he or she." Let it be clearly understood, however, that the term "he" as used here applies as much to women board members, chairmen, executives, and staff as to men. Women may be exceptions to many rules but not to those laid down in this book.

"DELICATE BALANCES"

As this chapter has shown, the board is a far-from-simple mechanism. Apparent contradictions are inherent in its very nature, and delicate balances must constantly be achieved if it is to succeed. One might almost say that boards could never have been invented if it were not so evident that in many fields and at many different times, they have been invented afresh. They might almost seem unworkable if it were not for the fact that they are at work everywhere.

CHAPTER TWO

The Human Resources
of the Board

PEOPLE are selected for board membership in three major ways. They are invited to join by those who are already on the board. They are chosen by some outside appointing authority. They are chosen by the people through the process of election. But, although these three methods are the most common, there are others as well, and even the three basic methods are subject to a variety of approaches. Sometimes, for example, a mayor or governor may have the legal power to appoint but, in practice, chooses only those people who are recommended by the present members of the board. Also, a single board may employ several different kinds of selection processes.[1]

---

[1] The board of Cornell University, in 1947, had 15 self-perpetuating members, 10 elected by alumni, 5 appointed by the Governor, 8 public officials serving *ex officio*, the eldest male descendant of Ezra Cornell, and one member elected by the state Grange. (Thomas H. Hamilton, "The Control of Universities in

In most cases the decision as to who shall be on a board rests primarily on the judgment of some individual who has the appointive power or some group which has the responsibility to make a selection. Nominating and slate-making committees are examples of such groups. One purpose of this chapter is to suggest some policies and procedures which might guide such an individual or group, which, for simplicity's sake, is here called the *selecting authority*.

Once a member is chosen for a board, he must learn about the policies and procedures which guide its work. The second purpose of this chapter, therefore, is to suggest the best ways to help him gain the understanding he needs.

1. WHY PEOPLE JOIN BOARDS

People always have mixed motives for what they do. Even the shrewdest analyst could not disentangle and label all the reasons why people want to be on boards. Donald McCarty has probably come as close to a complete list as anyone.[2] He conducted lengthy interviews, lasting from two to five hours each, with fifty-two school board members who came from communities of markedly different types. He asked each person not only why he had joined the board but also why he thought his colleagues had done so. In-

the United States." Unpublished doctoral dissertation, The University of Chicago, 1947, p. 23.)

[2] "Motives for Seeking School Board Membership" (Unpublished doctoral dissertation, The University of Chicago, 1959).

terestingly enough, there were relatively few differences between the two lists.

From these interviews, it was possible to identify twenty-one different reasons why people thought they had joined school boards. Of these, the most frequent were the following:

Felt it to be a civic duty	46%
Persuaded or pressured by friends	38%
Interest in educational matters	29%
Opportunity to learn something new	17%
Recognition, honor, prestige	14%
Satisfactions received from PTA work	10%
Disapproved of the way schools were being run	10%

People being as they are, many of those McCarty interviewed gave complex answers. It proved to be quite possible, for example, for someone to say he joined the board partly because of a sense of civic duty and partly because of a desire to achieve prestige.

When McCarty sorted his fifty-two persons into groups in terms of what seemed to him to be their major motivation, he arrived at the following interesting analysis:

Those who were extremely altruistic	10%
Those who were apparently altruistic	36%
Those who were partially self-interested	44%
Those who were extremely self-interested	10%

These findings will come as no great surprise to

anyone who knows board members or, for that matter, people! Perhaps it is disturbing to find in this sample that those who are partially or extremely self-interested slightly outnumber those who are altruistic. But if this fact is generally true, it had better be recognized, particularly since it offers clues as to how to get and keep effective people on a board. Whoever selects the members for a given board should begin by thinking about why people might want to be on it. The more realistically a selecting authority faces the matter of motivation, the better will be its chances of finding effective people and convincing them that they should accept membership.

It might be argued that a board should have only members who are altruistically motivated. Happy is the board which can take this stand and hold to it! Most boards are not in such a fortunate position. To get the kinds of members who will do the agency or association the most good, the selecting authority must often choose at least some people who join for reasons of self-interest, even if it is only so innocent a motive as the desire for recognition or prestige. After all, the distillation of absolutely pure motives is far from easy. As Pascal observed a great many years ago, "Those who write against vanity wish to have the glory of having written well, and those who read them wish to have the glory of reading well, and I who write this have the same desire, and maybe also those who read this."[3]

---
[3] *Pensées*, II.

Proper attention to motivation is also essential after people have joined a board. Many board members with only self-interested motives at the start may later achieve a broader and more altruistic point of view. The chairman who wants to create a sense of responsibility on the part of his fellow members must approach them in terms of their own interests and concerns. If he makes his appeal on the basis of a single motive—lecturing them on their civic duty, for instance—he will reach only those members who identify themselves with that motive. The other members of the board will merely feel guilty—and guiltiness is not conducive to a positive feeling toward the board. But if the chairman accepts existing motives and acts skillfully and subtly in terms of them, giving the members a sense of satisfaction about what they do for the agency or association, he can gradually build responsibility on the part of individuals and enthusiasm on the part of the group.

The aim should be the strengthening of altruistic motives, for a board never becomes fully mature until its members are bound together by a devotion to some cause outside themselves. This sense of service does not grow automatically. It is created chiefly as people put something of themselves into the work of the board, becoming more and more involved in its activities, and seeing the tangible accomplishments which are a definite result. The first efforts of a good many board members must be motivated by reasons which are at least partially self-interested. It is only later that such members subordinate their own interests to those of the agency or association which the board serves.

2. WHO SHOULD BE ON A BOARD?

The opportunity to establish a wholly new board occurs rarely. For present purposes, however, it is useful to consider what happens when this opportunity does occur. In such a case, the selecting authority usually does not start by considering particular names. It begins by thinking about the basic nature of the board itself and considering what kinds of people should be placed on it.

A first question has to do with the basic traits which *all* board members should possess. Most people, as they think about board membership, assume that ideally it should involve men and women who possess certain personality attributes. Among them, perhaps the most common would be these: a commitment to the importance of the service or function with which the new board is to be concerned; a respected position in the community; intelligence; courage; a capacity for growth; a capacity to influence favorable public opinion in important areas in the community; a willingness to serve; and an ability to work with others. A selecting authority may find it possible to bring such a list of traits forward for discussion, but sometimes this procedure leads only to embarrassment, and it is better to leave the list implicit rather than explicit. Most of those with selection responsibilities do have such a list of traits more or less clearly in mind, however, as the discussion of particular candidates reveals.

The question facing a selecting authority is what kinds of representation should be included and how wide the range of such representation should be. The essential nature of the board indicates that it should include as many different kinds of people as is practicable in terms of the immediate situation, since the problems with which boards are faced should be viewed from as many different angles as possible. No flat rules about representation can be given, however. For example, some people might argue that all boards should have representatives from both sexes, but a man would be as out of place on the board of a Junior League as would a woman on the board of a Rotary club. Some very successful boards include a relatively narrow range of interests; the boards of some of the outstanding private American universities illustrate this point.

The matter of representation must be left to the judgment of the selecting authority, but it should put down in concrete terms precisely what it is looking for. When it does so, the following kinds of factors are usually brought forth for consideration in addition to the general traits already stated:

(a) *Important elements in the constituency.* In a public board, it is sometimes thought necessary that the major religious, ethnic, and economic groups be represented. In a private welfare board, it may be necessary to identify those who are likely to support the work, and to draw board members from each major group within that constituency.

(b) *Important elements in the clientele.* The board of a private school may be made up of parents of children in the school; the exact nature of the clientele, therefore, is important in selecting members of the board. In the establishment of a settlement house, it may well be useful to have representation from among the people who will be served in the neighborhood.

(c) *Sex.* With rather obvious exceptions, such as those already noted, it is usually wise to have both men and women on a board.

(d) *Age.* Most boards need to have a spread in the age of board members. The older group has the experience, the wisdom, and usually the economic resources. The middle group carries the major positions of active responsibility in society, and can assist the agency or association in effectively relating itself to the community. The younger group has energy and drive; also it needs to be prepared for greater subsequent responsibility.

(e) *Special capacities needed on the board.* Each agency or association has certain problems whose solution requires the specialized assistance of one or more board members. Among the major problem areas are personnel policies, investment, political contacts, money raising, legal matters, building and

25

grounds, and public relations. People may well be appointed in terms of their capacity to assist in these specific ways.

(f) *Location of residence.* Public boards often require membership from the different parts of the city, or county, or state, or nation. National boards of private agencies or associations usually set up their selection procedures to draw representation from each major region.

(g) *Relative experience in board processes.* A board may need to involve both those who are highly experienced in board procedure and those who are serving their first apprenticeship in board activity.

Practice varies from one kind of agency or association to another as to whether the executive should belong to the board. In business, it is universally accepted that he should be a member. In some other fields, he is not chosen for such a position. In general, the sounder view appears to be that he should not be a member. If the board and the executive are to operate most effectively in terms of their respective functions, there is good reason to keep a structural distinction between them. The executive can, in any case, be only a special kind of board member, and to have him serve in that capacity confuses somewhat the relationship between him and the board.

These bases of membership overlap, but each is distinct from the others. There may well be other categories which should be considered. But, though categories are useful—indeed, essential—the selecting authority must not let itself become entrapped by them. Some outstanding potential board members simply cannot be fitted into slots. There is said to be an Arabian proverb which holds that mankind is divided into three classes: those who are immovable, those who are movable, and those who move. A nominating committee wants to be sure to get those who move. It also wants some people who are generally competent and who will find their particular niches later. And the possibility that some potential board member might bequeath a million dollars to the agency can be a highly relevant factor in his selection, even though it may not be discreet to include this fact in any formal list of board requirements.

3. HOW TO SELECT NEW BOARD MEMBERS

Most selecting authorities face a more complicated task than the creation of a new board. They must consider how to add new board members to an already existing group. Since each board has a life and a personality of its own, its nature is altered with each new member just as surely as a chemical compound is changed by pouring in a new substance, or a recipe is modified by including a new ingredient. Adding a new board member is not a simple matter of arithmetic: it puts a complex human being into interaction with a complex social entity. Usually if the result is unhappy, it is hard to remedy the situation. The chemical cannot be extracted, the in-

27

gredient taken out, or the board member's influence removed. Nothing will ever be the same again.

One common way of trying to cover up past mistakes in selecting board members is simply to enlarge the board. The reasoning seems to be, "The people now on the board aren't working out well; let's get some new people to see whether they can't make things better." Sometimes it *is* necessary to enlarge a board, but the ineffectiveness of the present membership is not very good grounds for doing so. The net result is often a big ineffective board rather than a small ineffective board—and ineffectiveness grows worse as it grows larger. More than that, the integration of the board will suffer. It can no longer act as a proper deliberative body, but becomes diffuse and un-co-ordinated and finally unable to carry on its proper functions.

The task of a selecting authority in finding good new people to add to a board, therefore, must be taken with the utmost seriousness. Many appointing or nominating bodies have found it profitable, in this situation, to use the following procedure:

First, the selecting authority makes its own analysis of the desirable composition of the board, acting precisely as though that board were being created afresh, and taking into account such factors as those identified in the previous section. Such an analysis may already be in existence as a legacy from an earlier effort of the same sort, in which case the selecting authority should consider what revisions it wishes to

28

make. This new examination should be keenly an-
alytical and never take past judgments as being final.
For example, one Red Cross committee in Wisconsin
discovered, upon re-examination of its list of criteria,
that for many years the chapter had been without representation from two important segments in the community, and that these omissions not only affected
the ideal broad representation desired but caused
the chapter to miss out on some very explicit technical assistance which it needed.

Second, the selecting authority determines how
well the present members represent the various categories which have been included. This process must
usually be a confidential one, involving as it does the
making of judgments about people, not the least of
which is estimating the age of the feminine members
of the board.

Third, the selecting authority decides what categories are underrepresented or not included at all in
the present membership. When it does so, it will
have a clear idea of what kinds of people it should be
looking for.

A useful device for carrying out these three steps
is to set up a two-way grid of the sort presented in
Figure 1. Here is illustrated the example of a fictitious Home for Destitute University Professors. The
nominating committee has chosen only four major
criteria for this board though it might well have
added many more. (1) There should be a spread in
the ages of the members of the board. (2) The board

29

Figure 1
Analysis of Present Board Members of the Home for Destitute University Professors

Criteria	Present Board Members									Potential Board Members		
	A	B	C	D	E	F	G	H	I	X	Y	Z
AGE												
under 35 years of age	x											
from 35 to 50 years of age		x					x					
over 50 years of age			x	x	x	x		x	x			
RESIDENCE												
north side of city	x	x			x	x		x				
west side of city			x				x		x			
south side of city				x								
SEX												
men			x	x	x		x	x	x			
women	x	x				x						
RESPONSIBILITIES												
personnel	x	x										
investment						x						
benefit			x				x	x				
contributions				x	x							
legal	x											
building		x				x						

30

should represent the whole city. (3) The board should be evenly divided so far as men and women are concerned. (4) There are certain responsibilities which must be cared for by people who have special competencies.

The board has twelve members, each with a four-year term. The board itself selects the new members. All three of the persons retiring this year have said that they cannot accept renomination. Acting in strictest confidence, the nominating committee has analyzed the nine remaining members, including, of course, those who are on the committee itself. The results are shown in Figure 1.

What kinds of people should the three new board members be? Inspection of the grid suggests some answers. Two should be under 35 years of age, and one should be in the next higher age bracket. Two or three should be from the south side. Probably all three should be men. The legal responsibilities are underrepresented and so are those which have to do with the building.

The nominating committee must still find the people who fit into these categories, but it will be helped a great deal by the fact that it knows what it is looking for. Naturally enough it will not be just any young, male, south-side lawyer who will be suitable, but to have established a framework helps to define the field. With the choice narrowed, the job is like any other search. The committee thinks about its own contacts and invites the help of those who might be useful. Eventually the right candidate will come into view and, because the committee knows what it wants, it will be able to recognize him.

4. HOW TO INVITE PEOPLE TO BE ON A BOARD

Once the prospective board member has been identified, he must be asked to serve. Sometimes the selecting authority has the power to make a direct request of him. Sometimes he must be asked for permission to submit his name to the board itself or another source of appointment. Sometimes he must be urged to stand for election, either opposed or unopposed. In all these cases, someone must get in touch with the prospective board member.

Education of a new board member starts at the moment of invitation, and much of his later viewpoint begins to be fixed then. One of the chief causes of later lethargy on the part of many board members is poor handling of this initial interview. All too frequently the invitation is offered in a casual, haphazard way, which places the board activity in the wrong light from the beginning. At worst, the prospective board member may be assured that he won't have to give much time, that the agency or association has few problems which need solution, that board service is chiefly a matter of coming to a few lunches a year which he can feel free to skip if more pressing engagements conflict, and that he will not be expected to carry any particular responsibilities but just be a voting member of the whole board. If these facts are true, the board cannot be very important; if they are not true, the new board member begins his service with a misconception.

An invitation to join a board should never be hurried and never be casual. It should take place in a personal interview in which there is plenty of time for discussion and, if possible, in a pleasant social situation. The prospective board member should be told the purpose of the interview at the time it is arranged. The invitation should be issued by whoever is most likely to get a favorable answer. This assignment might be given, for example, to a present board member who is a friend of the person being invited.

The interview itself should be a clear and concrete presentation of the work of the agency or association, the major problems it now faces, the general responsibility of a board member, and the particular role the desired person is expected to fulfill. If the selecting authority has done its work properly, it will know precisely why it is asking this person to join the board and it is well to tell him so.

If these suggestions are followed, the desired person will be far more likely to accept than if he is invited hastily or casually or if he is told that he will have to undertake few responsibilities. The knowledge that the selecting authority has very specific reasons for choosing a board member will make him feel more like accepting; everyone likes to feel wanted. Then, too, most people know that being on a board is not a responsibility to be taken lightly and they are not at all fooled by the suggestion that they will have little work to do if they accept. The prospective board member will respect a selecting authority which knows what it is doing and this respect will be transferred to the board itself.

Many prospective board members do not need persuasion at all, but are only too eager to accept. They may, in fact, have been straining every muscle and pulling every string in the effort to be chosen. When this is the case, there is always a temptation to take the easy way out and save time in issuing the invitation. But as has already been pointed out, the moment when people first begin to identify themselves with a board is the crucial time for beginning their education and establishing their orientation. The new board member may have been so dazzled by the aura of the board that he has been blinded to the fact that his membership will involve him in a number of new responsibilities. The interview of invitation should therefore be as carefully handled for someone who is eager to accept as for one who may be reluctant. One must never take "yes" for an answer, until that "yes" comes from knowledge.

If the answer to the invitation is "no" even after such an interview, it is comforting to realize that at least a constructive piece of community relations has been accomplished. The prospective board member will have been given information about the program, will know that he was wanted, and will have sensed

34

that the selecting authority (and probably the board itself) knows its business. He is probably an influential person (or else he would not have been invited) and it is important to have influential people aware of the work of the agency or the association.

Some people want to accept, but only in terms of certain conditions or restrictions. They ask to be excused in advance from raising money, or coming to board meetings, or taking on special assignments. Unless it is so crucial to have the particular person that there is virtually no other choice, such conditions should not be accepted. The selecting authority may not really be able to exempt new board members from their usual responsibilities, in which case the agreement to do so becomes a false promise with the inevitable resentment that always follows. But the reason for not accepting conditions goes much deeper. The board is, after all, collectively and wholly responsible; its members cannot arbitrarily excuse themselves (and hence cannot excuse a colleague) from the exercise of their duty. Those who try to do so remind one of Uncle Dudley who was taken for his first airplane ride at the age of 84. When he landed, he was asked how he had liked the experience. "Well," he allowed, "it was right interesting. But I'll have to admit I never did let my full weight down." The members of a board let their full weight down when they join, and it is useless for them to pretend that they still have an independent influence over the law of gravity.

5. HOW TO INDUCT NEW BOARD MEMBERS

As soon as the new member has been chosen, his introduction to the board begins. At this point, his initial interest must be used to broaden his knowledge and to deepen his commitment. If his introduction to the board is not effective, there is a good chance that he will never become fully involved. The importance of an effective induction probably does not need to be further stressed, nor are the possible techniques obscure. As an experienced board chairman once remarked, "Everybody really knows what to do; they just don't take time to do it." Still it may be useful to list and describe briefly some of the widely used methods of introducing new board members to their responsibilities. A board which wishes to improve its practice may choose from these or other methods those which are best for its situation:

(*a*) Immediately after his selection, the new board member should receive a welcome and an offer of assistance from both the chairman and the executive. The welcome may be given in a personal visit, a telephone call, or, if need be, in a letter. This practice will make the new member feel that he is important to the board, that he will not be neglected or allowed to float until he finds for himself what he is expected to contribute, and that he will know where to turn for knowledge about the agency or association.

(*b*) Some board chairmen supplement this welcome

by arranging a special conference with the new board member; sometimes the executive also attends this conference. Its purpose is to permit the chairman to make certain that the new member understands the work of the agency or association and the particular responsibilities he is supposed to undertake. Also the new member may be given background information about the other members of the board. His questions should be encouraged and every effort made to be certain that the environment is permissive enough to stimulate his curiosity and overcome whatever shyness he may feel.

(c) Some boards are so large that this special conference must be turned into a group meeting which includes all new members of the board simultaneously. Some boards have even gone so far as to set up a regular orientation class which meets several times and which is so structured as to give a very complete introduction to the program, the board, the executive, and the staff.

(d) Some board chairmen also schedule a later orientation conference after the new board members have had several months of experience and are better equipped to raise questions.

(e) In some boards, an experienced member acts as a special sponsor for each new member, making sure that he has all the information he needs, that he has been introduced to the existing members, and that he has someone to whom to turn for the answers to questions. The sponsor technique has the advantage

37

of saving the time of the chairman and the executive, and of allowing the process of induction to last over a period of time. Also the sponsor gets a re-education!

(*f*) Some boards which recognize the value of good social relationships arrange an informal occasion at which the entire board can meet the new members. This kind of social affair permits new people to become acquainted with their future associates as personalities, and tends to start the relationship on a relaxed basis.

(*g*) The board chairman must be sure that the new member has a careful and thorough introduction to the other members of the board. The normal social introduction is not enough. One may know the name of one's future associates on a board and still not know anything at all about them, their backgrounds and interests, and their special contributions to the board. A relaxed and effective social relationship cannot be built except on the basis of such understanding.

(*h*) Many boards control physical facilities. The new member should be sure to visit these premises and see them in use. This visit will be of great help in understanding the program and in giving the new member a sense of the reality of the operating situation.

(*i*) Many boards use the practice of placing a packet of materials describing the agency or association and the board in the hands of new members. Such a packet might include the board manual, the latest annual report and budget, an organizational chart of the staff, descriptive literature on the program, a set of minutes of the past year, and any other relevant documents.

(*j*) Some chairmen try to see that new members are provided with literature which describes the board functions undertaken by the kind of agency or association which the board controls. A new board member of a YMCA, for example, might be given pamphlets or books which describe current thinking about YMCA programing.

(*k*) Many manuals have been prepared for special types of board members. Such assistance is available, for example, for the trustees of hospitals, schools, universities, libraries, and welfare agencies. A few current books in these various fields are listed in the Bibliography on page 168. The relevant books might be made available by a chairman to all new members. It is hoped, too, that *The Effective Board* will be useful in helping to induct new members.

(*l*) In some fields of work, such as public education or library service, there are special associations for board members, with annual meetings, publications, and other activities. If such an association exists, the board chairman may well encourage all new members to join it and participate in its program.

(*m*) In some places, special institutes and conferences for board members are held. These may be general meetings for all board members, or special activities for those who serve on particular kinds of boards.

(*n*) One of the most effective methods of introducing a new member to a board is to give him a job to do. Actual participation is the surest stimulus to interest. When the new member has made a contribution of time and effort to the board he has become personally involved in its work. In choosing this first assignment, the board chairman might well keep in mind the following criteria: it should be something which the new member wants to do or which has its pleasant aspects; it should not be too arduous or demand too much detailed knowledge; it should be carried on in association with other board members; and it should be an activity for whose successful completion the new board member can be given recognition and praise.

There are other techniques and good practices, but those already mentioned will serve to indicate both the importance of effective induction and how it may be achieved. A chairman who fails to set up a proper procedure for this purpose and who later complains that the members do not take enough interest in the work of the board is like the man (in Abraham Lincoln's story) who murdered his mother and father and then threw himself on the mercy of the court on the ground that he was an orphan.

6. THE CONTINUING EDUCATION OF THE BOARD MEMBER

Once the board member has been initiated, he must not be allowed to stagnate. His work for the board should provide a continuing stimulus, as will membership in board members' associations. But the chairman of the board cannot leave matters to chance. He must be aware of the need for developing the abilities of the board members more rapidly than by letting nature take its course. In doing so, he must be subtle, for his role is not defined as that of a teacher, and, in fact, he is really more of a fellow student—even though first among equals—than an instructor. He should remember Alexander Pope's maxim:

> Men must be taught as if you taught them not,
> And things unknown proposed as things forgot.[4]

The first task of the board chairman is to see that everything goes well during his own term of office, but he can never forget that the board is continuous in its influence and that he must strengthen it so that in later years, it will be even better than it is in his administration. One of the ways he does this is by making the board members better able to carry out their responsibilities. As soon as he knows that he will be assuming the chairmanship, he should reflect about each separate board member, weighing his potential for growth so far as the board is concerned.

---

[4] *An Essay on Criticism,* III.

41

Then, in carrying on the work of the board, and particularly in making assignments, the board chairman should keep in mind how he may best help to develop that potential. He may, for example, appoint to a committee a person who might become its chairman later on, or who would profit from the experience of working with its present chairman, or who needs to understand more about the subject matter with which that committee is concerned. Many other possibilities of the same sort exist; a number are suggested by the various procedures presented throughout this book. As the board chairman thinks about how he can help the members to develop, he will discover that he has far more opportunities than he first realized.

The exccutive also plays a significant role in the continuing education of the board member. It is his special responsibility to keep the board informed about the work of the agency or association and the field of activity which it represents. Thus a county health director should keep his board informed about the program in the county and also about recent advances in public health which have implications for the local program. Sometimes executives are shy, or afraid of the board, or reluctant to take its time. In such a case, the board chairman must make every effort to create opportunities for the executive to inform the board, and encourage the executive to take advantage of those opportunities.

A central feature of most board meetings should be

the opportunity provided to the executive to make a report on the program. Many boards fall so much into the habit of dealing with organizational, financial, and procedural matters that they never give proper time to understanding the primary function of the agency or association itself. The program report is put as the last item on the agenda, so that the time of the meeting or the patience of the members is exhausted before the executive has a chance to speak. A few hurried remarks are then delivered while the board members surreptitiously consult their watches or steal away. The board chairman and the executive must plan the meeting so that this unhappy result does not occur.

Above all else, the executive has the responsibility to make the report interesting. Statistics are essential but they should be personalized with typical cases, problems, successes, failures, interesting new developments, and the results of significant research. It is this kind of lively and absorbing personal detail which interests the executive and staff and sustains their enthusiasm. They should communicate to the board some of the life and vitality of their work, not distill all the human essence out of it.

Reports at meetings are useful in informing the whole board, but other devices may also be used. Some have already been mentioned in the previous section. Others are as follows:

(a) A program of continuous stimulation by reading, in which new books in the field or copies of in-

43

teresting pamphlet material are circulated to all board members.

(*b*) Visits to other agencies in the same field of work. For example, the board of one institution may find it illuminating to visit the program of another similar agency or to have a joint meeting with its board.

(*c*) Service to over-all co-ordinating groups. In some fields of work, most notably welfare and health, councils have been established to co-ordinate the activities of various agencies of the same sort. Such councils usually are under lay control and an important part of their work is done by the board members of the various agencies. This work has value in providing perspective for the board member concerning his own agency.

(*d*) Presentation of cases by the executive or staff to the board. In this method, an outstanding or interesting example of the agency's work is selected and described to the board at a regular board meeting or on some special occasion. At least one board in the family service field has established a regular monthly meeting for this purpose; new board members are expected to go to every session during their first year of service, and "old" board members go at least twice a year.

These particular methods are merely illustrative. Most members of boards join them out of either a generalized or a specialized desire to be of service.

They come on the board because they believe in the program. So far as possible that belief should be constantly reinforced by greater knowledge.

7. THE ATTITUDE OF THE BOARD MEMBER

The board member needs more than knowledge and interest: he must also approach his responsibilities with the proper attitude. His viewpoint may be influenced by the chairman of the board or by the other members. Chiefly, however, it is a product of his own effort. Though the various aspects of this attitude are implicit throughout this book, it is well to make them explicit.

The board member should place the larger interests of the agency or association above personal or factional concerns. As McCarty's research showed, people belong to boards for all kinds of reasons. Occasionally boards fall prey to the selfish interests of the few or the many, to schisms and cliques, or to domination by a self-seeking individual or group. Often, too, choices must be made between two courses of action, one of which seems to lead toward breadth and the other toward narrowness. In such cases, the board member's responsibility is always toward the larger purpose. Honorable people can, of course, disagree about which course of action truly serves the larger purpose, but it is always their responsibility to make their choice on that basis.

The board member must serve as an effective intermediary between the agency or association and any special group he represents. He may have been chosen because he comes from a certain social or economic segment of the community, or lives in a special district, or believes in a particular creed, or belongs to a racial or ethnic group. In such cases, he will ordinarily feel a sense of responsibility to those whom he regards as his own constituents. But even though he may reflect their wishes and their attitudes on the board, he cannot be governed by them. When he takes part in the deliberations of the board, he has taken his place in a new social context where his responsibility is to the larger purposes of the agency or association. There he must be governed by the considerations which can emerge only when those who represent different backgrounds discuss and debate the issues together. As Edmund Burke put it almost two hundred years ago, the representative must concern himself with "reason and judgment, and not . . . inclination; and what sort of reason is that in which the determination precedes the discussion, in which one set of men deliberate and another decide, and where those who form the conclusion are . . . distant from those who hear the arguments?"[5] The precise responsibility of the board member to his constituency on the one hand and the board on the other is not easy to define, as centuries of debate on the point show. He must be governed by the particular situa-

---

[5] Quoted in *Materials on American National Government,* eds., John M. Swarthout and Ernest R. Bartley (New York: Oxford University Press, 1952), p. 254.

tion which confronts him, trying his best to discharge his obligation in both directions.

The board member must support the board as long as he remains a part of it. Unlike Uncle Dudley, he has let his full weight down. Within the board itself, he may champion particular causes, he may express displeasure if the vote goes against him, and he may take a strong position opposing others on the board who disagree with him. He does real harm, however, if he criticizes the program openly or even permits outsiders to know that he does not support it. The executive has the right to expect that the board will stand behind him in this fashion. He, in turn, has an equal obligation to support the agency's or association's policies as long as he is employed by it.

The board member should expect to be informed. Perhaps nothing else so hampers effective decisions as the failure on the part of board members to understand the issues involved. The failure is not always one of negligence. Often the board member who does not really understand an issue hesitates to let the other members know that fact for fear they will think him ignorant. Actually one of the chief rights and responsibilities of a board member is to ask questions. He will often discover, when he does so, that he is not alone in his ignorance and, in fact, the question he fears may sound naïve will often put the whole discussion on a sounder basis.

The board member must insist upon full discussion of each issue. The board cannot use its best judg-

47

ment unless there has been an opportunity to examine matters fully. A suitable motto might well be a line from Gilbert and Sullivan's *The Gondoliers:* "Calm cool deliberation disentangles every knot." In achieving this happy result, the board member must insist that decisions shall not be rushed. Here, too, the asking of questions is important, since it is one of the best weapons against hasty or highhanded action. If the chairman or the executive or a committee or a clique or even the rest of the board itself seems bent on a course of procedure the board member regards as ill-considered or unwise, he may well find that his best recourse is not to deliver a challenge but to ask a question, and if need be, to ask more than one. Who can deny his right to be informed? To be sure the questions should be discerning and they should not be malicious in intent. If they spring from a genuine motive of service, if they are honestly put, and if they do not descend to the level of hectoring cross-examination, they are sure to contribute to the effectiveness of the board. Socrates did rather well with this technique and his is good company to be in— at least up to the point of the eventual hemlock.

A CONCLUDING NOTE

The main idea of this chapter is that a board can be no better than its members. As we have seen, the matter of selection goes deeper than the choice of the "right" people. There are indeed some men and women who, because of innate capacity or wealth or po-

48

sition in a community, would be welcome additions to most boards. The major choice, however, should be made in terms of those who are "right" for a particular board, who can strengthen it, and give it what it needs. It is important, also, to take advantage of the fact that human beings are capable of continuous intellectual growth. Neither the choice of board members nor their increased knowledge should be left to chance. Later chapters in this book describe the best ways to organize and carry out the work of the board, but all such matters are vitally influenced by the caliber and depth of understanding of the human resources of the board.

CHAPTER THREE

Improving the Organization
of the Board

*I*n a medical school, the student is taught both anatomy and physiology. He examines the structure of
the human body as well as its various functions. But
always he knows that he is dealing with the same essential unity. The heart is a separate organ and its
nature and operation may be studied as such, but it
beats only when it is a part of a living human being.

This chapter deals with the anatomy of boards, and
the next two chapters with their physiology. Where
unity of treatment of a topic would be destroyed by
too rigid a separation, however, the fundamental distinction has been abandoned. The three chapters
make up a single unit, for the board, like the body,
has an essential unity. Each aspect of structure and of
operation is here singled out for analysis and study,
but in practice all aspects must mesh together if the
board is to be whole and healthy.

8. THE BOARD'S CONCERN FOR ITS OWN ORGANIZATION

The interrelationship of structure and function needs emphasis because many board members misunderstand it in their constant quest for a perfect organization. All problems cannot be solved by structure alone. This fact is demonstrated clearly in any national association in which authorities have designed a master plan for the boards of local chapters. Such boards, though they operate with identical structures, will always vary widely in their effectiveness.

All that any organizational plan can do is to provide a framework which makes relationships among people more logical. The framework must be operated by the people involved, and they will quickly make it conform to their own capacities and purposes. Every organization chart is an allegory whose maker asserts that conditions in life conform to the lines and rectangles he has drawn. But the allegory is always breaking down; every position in an agency or association is defined by the shape of the person who holds it and not by any rectangle, however neatly drawn. An intense and continuing concern with structure alone is a sure sign of danger.

A board is never the sole master of its own organization. The outside influences brought to bear on it vary from situation to situation, but, in general, they include laws, the wishes of the constituency, constitutional provisions, traditions, commitments made to other agencies or associations, and regulations established by some higher authority such as a national association. Every board has some power over its own structure, however, and if its members feel that this power is not sufficient, they usually know how to try to change the outside conditions which restrict them. Remedies may be difficult to apply (for example, it is hard to change a law), but they are clear enough.

Ideally a board should operate so perfectly and so naturally that its members never have to think about its structure. Like most ideals, this one is hard to achieve. Organization is merely the way by which people relate themselves to one another so as to achieve their common purposes. In a one-man grocery store, the proprietor does everything, but, as soon as he hires a helper, there must be some division of responsibility. Only a one-man board would need have no concern at all with structure, and a one-man board is a contradiction in terms—though such a board is not wholly unknown in practice!

So far as possible, boards should devote their time to shaping policy and furthering program, but this result can be achieved only if the members of the board are effectively related to one another. A poorly organized board can continue to exist, but it cannot thrive, for it has no way to mobilize or channel the energies of its members. Either systematically or whenever problems of relationship begin to appear, someone—the whole board, a committee, or an individual—must consider whether the structure itself can be at fault. When such a review is necessary, it usually takes place in terms of the matters dealt with in this chapter.

9. CAREFUL RECORDS

Members usually have only a limited amount of time to give to the board. It is essential that this time be devoted, so far as possible, to the important rather than the trivial, to policy-making rather than routine decisions, and to the performance of service for the program rather than discussion of organizational details. The best way to achieve these goals is to define functions and relationships very clearly—and in writing—and to keep careful records of the decisions of the board.

It seems a paradox to say that a board will be helped to do its major work if it takes time away from that work to think about mechanics and structure. But the situation is like that of the woodsman who said that if he had only ten minutes to cut down a tree, he'd use the first two minutes to sharpen his axe. Board members who have found themselves caught in endless wrangles about whether a committee had a right to make a certain decision or what the board really *did* decide on a certain point, or who have found themselves at meeting after meeting making separate judgments on similar kinds of problems will readily agree that clarity of function, exactness of record, and firmness of policy make the board's axe a great deal sharper.

53

Usually a board should have at least three kinds of written records.

The first major record is its *constitution and by-laws*. Sometimes these two are separate but often they are combined in a single document. The constitution states the general purpose of the agency or association and defines the basic conditions of existence of the board. The by-laws are rules established to guide the procedure of the board. Generally speaking, private boards have much more control over their constitutions and by-laws than do public boards. In this latter case there may, indeed, be an extensive body of law which defines and restricts the structure of the board.

Boards are so diverse in their patterns that there can be no master list of the items which should be present in a satisfactory constitution or set of by-laws. A number of the books suggested in the Bibliography go into this matter in some detail so far as various kinds of boards are concerned. Such books will be helpful to anyone who feels a need to construct or revise basic documents. Also, many boards have one or more persons who are experienced in preparing and using such documents and there are often a number of examples of constitutions and by-laws readily available in the community. In general, there are at least two rules which should be observed:

The first rule is that care should be taken to construct as complete and suitable a set of basic documents as is possible. This may well be a task for a special committee. In the matter of what to include, there can be errors of both omission and commission, too little and too much. The committee can be given little general help here, other than the admonition: include everything essential and nothing superfluous. It must use its judgment in determining both what to include, and what to say about the topics which are included.

The second rule is that the basic documents should be kept up to date. A board always has a particular responsibility to recommend changes in the constitution to its constituency; it also has the obligation to keep its by-laws current. The best practice is to make an annual review; the chairman can do this himself or he can ask a committee to do it. If changes are called for, they can be made as needed. If an annual review is not undertaken, the basic documents will grow more and more antiquated and soon come to have little relationship to what the board is doing—and this is a state of affairs which may lead to explosive results.

The second major record of a board is its *statement of policies*. From time to time boards make decisions about recurrent problems or issues. These decisions should be recorded and made available to all who need to know them. In some situations, a simple list of policies is enough; in others, particularly in boards which are responsible for large and complex matters, it is important to have a codification of policies which essentially becomes a body of law for the agency or association involved. Usually the executive plays an important role in drafting, recommending, and recording policies, for they guide the program he administers.

Since policies are so important, it is perplexing to note that many—and perhaps most—boards do not bother to keep a separate written record of their policy decisions. The importance of doing so is not merely a matter of logic; its value has been demonstrated by research. Richard E. Whalen, Jr., in a study of school boards, has shown that boards with written policies are significantly more effective than boards without them.[1]

The third major record of a board is made up of its *minutes,* not only those of the whole board, but also those of the committees and other groups which carry out special responsibilities at the wish of the board. Minutes are the indispensable record of the deliberations and decisions of a board. If they are not kept, confusion and conflict will almost inevitably result.

10. BOARD MANUALS

One of the most useful specific devices to help provide a sense of integration in a board is a manual. Essentially this is a document—preferably a loose-leaf notebook, to permit ready changes—which belongs

---

[1] Richard E. Whalen, Jr., "Effectiveness of Elected and Appointed Board Members" (Unpublished doctoral dissertation, Indiana University, Bloomington, Indiana, 1953).

to the board, but which is given to each member to hold during his tenure and which he is responsible for keeping up to date. If there is a limited number of securely and attractively bound copies, if they are numbered and issued, and if they must be returned at the close of a member's tenure, the board manual will be taken more seriously and will have a far greater effect than one which is casually developed and circulated.

A board manual should provide a ready reference tool for all members, and a means of training for new members. Catching a good likeness of a particular board on paper is a challenge, but it is one to which more and more boards are responding in their desire to improve their effectiveness. Each manual must be unique, if it is to picture its own board properly, but most manuals contain at least the following items: a description of the nature and program of the agency or association; the constitution; the by-laws; an annual schedule or plan of work of the board; a list of members with addresses and telephone numbers; a list of committees, with a statement of the function and membership of each; a statement of policies; an organization chart of the staff; the current budget; and a statement of any controlling legal provisions or major commitments to outside co-ordinating groups.

The writing of such a manual can well be made the assignment of a special committee. Often it is a good idea to appoint an experienced member as a chairman and to choose the other members from among those who have only recently joined the board. New members will not only be able to suggest more readily what they think they need to know, but also they will learn a great deal from the preparation of the manual.

The automatic revision of the manual, in which standard items are merely brought up to date, usually by the preparation of new loose-leaf sheets, can be carried out by the executive or a staff member whom he designates. Every chairman should, however, look at the manual with a critical eye at least annually to see if any items need to be added or omitted, and, every now and then, a more systematic rethinking of its nature and contents should be carried out by another special committee.

11. THE PROPER SIZE OF THE BOARD

Many authorities, dealing with a particular type of board, have suggested that it have a certain desirable size, or, at least, that its membership should fall somewhere within given limits. It has been suggested, to give a few examples, that a college board should have from seven to twelve members, that a school board should have from five to nine, and that a hospital board should have from seven to fifteen. However valid such rules may be for particular types, an examination of the range and variety of boards in American life soon leads to the conclusion that no such exact figures can have universal relevance. The matter of size must be left to the discretion of the board itself or to the outside authority which determines its structure.

In this situation, the best course of action is to consider the problems which a board will face if it becomes too large or too small. Here, at the extremes, are the real dangers to effective operation, and each board must decide what middle pathway it will take. Two general rules should be followed:

The first rule, which establishes a ceiling on the size of a board, is that *it should be small enough to act as a deliberative body*. A board is a collective entity and if it grows so large that it cannot meet and make decisions, it is no longer effective. The quality of the deliberation is endangered. In a very large board, the personal involvement of each member tends to decrease. People fail to assume the responsibilities which are properly theirs. Meetings become less frequent. The quality of the membership often declines, for the satisfactions of participation are not so great; also each member is relatively less important to the success of the board. Apathy grows. All these unhappy results, and others like them, are almost certain to result when a board grows so large that its members no longer find it possible to discuss issues easily together and to form an effective social unit.

When a board becomes too large, it often creates an "inner" board. This entity may be given some other name, such as "executive committee" but, out of sheer necessity, it becomes the active functioning board. The larger group then becomes, in a sense, a kind of constituency. Sometimes the creation of an "inner" board is the only practicable solution, but it is seldom a wholly desirable one, since it almost inevitably gives rise to problems of strain, conflict, overlapping jurisdiction, and misunderstanding. It is far better not to let the original board grow too large.

Occasionally boards seem from the outside to work very well even though they do have a large membership. Sometimes in such cases they are not true boards, though they have appropriated the name; they are groups of volunteer workers or casual sponsors, or auxiliary boards with limited responsibilities, or fictitious boards which exist to fulfill a public relations function. Sometimes there is an "inner" board which does the real work. Occasionally it is true that unusually effective leadership, the great prestige of the board, or the urgency of the work to be done permit a larger size—at least for a time. But such special conditions do not endure forever so that, in such cases, the problems presented by a large board are postponed, not solved.

The second rule, which establishes a floor to the size of the board, is that *it should be large enough to carry the necessary responsibilities*. If a board is too small, it runs into very serious problems. It cannot provide adequate policy guidance or assistance to the agency or association with which it is connected. It is too small to include all the groups that should be represented. It becomes too closely knit a group or it is paralyzed by factionalism. It has difficulty getting a quorum and therefore it is unable to operate at all or has to rely on individual decisions communicated by mail or telephone and arrived at with no opportunity for discussion or for clarification of issues.

In applying these two rules, it is useful to make the kind of analysis proposed in the grid presented in Chapter Two. Only by determining what functions should be performed and who will undertake them can it be decided how large a board must be. This process is never automatic. A nominating committee may realize that a particular man is needed on the board only because he will make a financial or political contribution or that a woman is included just because of her public relations value; these two persons can never be expected to come to board meetings or to take any other active part in the work of the board. Should they be left in and therefore enlarge the board perhaps toward the danger point? The simple answer is "no" but the practical answer must sometimes be "yes." Usually a committee (or any other authority concerned) should not concentrate its attention thus narrowly on two members only, but look at the total composition of the board and the responsibilities it must carry.

12. LENGTH OF TENURE ON THE BOARD

How long should a member stay on a board? This question may appear out of place in a chapter devoted to organization. The next two sections which suggest specific structural devices involving tenure will not be clear, however, unless they are introduced by a more general treatment of the subject.

Length of tenure is, in part, decided by the individual board member himself. People often wonder whether they should continue to serve, sometimes being stimulated to consider the matter because their present term is nearing its end. In any such case, the member should ask himself certain rather simple but searching questions:

(a) Do I continue to be strongly interested in the program?

(b) Am I providing effective support and assistance for the program?

(c) Do I have confidence in the effectiveness of the board itself?

(d) Am I at least as well qualified to serve as anybody who might take my place?

(e) Is my continuing membership likely to strengthen the caliber and unity of the board?

(f) Is the service I am performing on this board at least as significant as any other service to which I might devote the same time?

Such questions, since they are personal and require the use of judgment, do not produce precise answers, but they may be useful in helping a board member to arrive at a decision. If the answer to all or most of them is "yes," he should plan to continue on the board. If it is "no," he has a clear indication that it may be time for him to leave, as soon as he has completed his existing commitments and is able to withdraw with honor.

Length of tenure is also a matter of policy, decided by law, by an outside selecting authority, or by the board itself. As might be expected, practices vary widely. In many cases, tradition operates, and there seem to be no good reasons governing the length of time people stay on a board. "As it was in the beginning, is now, and ever shall be" appears to be the rule. As with other aspects of board structure and operation, however, it is usually wise at least to examine present practice to see whether the tradition should be continued or whether some better course of action might be followed.

Some boards have lifetime or indefinite tenure, either because the members are appointed on that basis or because it is expected that they will be reappointed as long as they are willing to serve. In this connection, one thinks at once of the boards of certain major private universities, hospitals, and welfare agencies, but there are many other institutions of all sorts which also have lifetime or indefinite tenure.

There are many arguments in favor of prolonged tenure, particularly for boards which are connected with large or complex agencies. In such cases, there is sometimes a wide variety of functions which need to be performed; the problems of the board are not easily mastered and remain to challenge the member even after years of service. Such a board may be capable of providing a continuing absorbing interest for its members—or, at least, most of them. Also, there may be a special need for stability and a long-range point of view which rises above immediate problems and issues and is concerned with continuity. The agency itself may be so specialized or have such diverse parts that there is need for accumulated general (rather than special) experience. Finally, some boards have such a high prestige that membership on them represents a crowning achievement in a civic or social career; and this fact alone is sufficient to keep people interested and to make their replacement an unwarranted threat to them and a difficult problem for the agency.

Lengthy tenure has its pronounced disadvantages as well. The chief difficulty is that it reduces the number of people who can have a place on the board; as a result, the breadth of representation may grow narrow, the past may dominate the present, there may be a lack of freshness of view, and policies may grow rigid and inflexible. Cliques may dominate both discussions and decisions. The interest of the members may wane. The outside appointing authorities (if there are such) may lose interest or a sense of involvement. If prolonged tenure is widespread in a community or a group of boards, there may be a cumulative bad effect in keeping a whole generation out of positions of leadership, with eventual disastrous results for the agencies concerned.

Brief tenure also has its advantages and its weaknesses. Simple agencies and associations may not have enough variety of program to hold the attention of their board members for more than a few years. In some boards, such as those of young people's associations, there is a need to involve and train as many individuals as possible. Sometimes there is a suspicion or fear of the board which makes a rapid turnover essential. (Samuel Adams once observed, in another connection, that "where annual elections end, tyranny begins," and some modern agencies and associations seem almost to believe him.) On some boards, there is much work to be done and people will not do it very long. In some cases, too, it is hard to get people to serve unless they can be promised short terms. Brief tenure also is sometimes said to have value in eliminating deadwood and providing a constant supply of new and fresh viewpoints.

Some of these values seem dubious to those who oppose short tenure for board members. A board can't be much good, they argue, if it is so distasteful that nobody wants to serve on it very long. Also, a short period of service does not provide enough time for the individual member to absorb what he needs to know, to make a substantial contribution, or to be prepared through experience for later major responsibilities.

These various arguments, taken all together, suggest that prolonged tenure and brief tenure are both appropriate under certain circumstances but, in general, the weight of the evidence is against either extreme. In length of service, the middle way is usually best. There must be a long enough tenure to provide continuity but a short enough tenure to secure constant freshness of viewpoint.

There is no automatic way to strike this happy balance, but two devices are frequently suggested to help a board achieve a proper practice so far as tenure is concerned. One is the establishment of definite terms of appointment; the other is the limitation of the number of consecutive terms each member may have. These two matters are related but distinct.

13. DEFINITE, OVERLAPPING TERMS

Most boards today have definite terms for their members with a provision for overlapping. (An illustration is that of a private club whose board has fifteen members, with three-year terms so staggered that one-third end each year.) The advantages of this arrangement (even to boards which, in practice, seem to have lifetime tenure) appear so obvious to many people that they are surprised to learn that a great many boards have never adopted it. Since this fact is true, it is well to summarize these advantages:

First, definite terms provide beginning and termination points for membership, thereby giving concreteness to board planning. It is possible for the board chairman, for example, to think more constructively about his committee assignments and the initiation of long-range plans with some certainty as to who will remain on the board to carry them out.

Second, definite, overlapping terms provide at once for continuity and for change. The rotation system should be so established that no more than one-half, and preferably no more than one-third, of the terms expire at a time.

Third, definite terms provide built-in motivation for those who want to stay on the board. The best way to be asked to serve a second term is to have been an active and valuable member during the first term.

Fourth, definite terms make it much easier to plan for a broad base of representation. The board cannot always contain at any one time all the kinds of people who have a concern with the program, but a suitable diversity can be arranged over a period of years.

Fifth, definite terms provide a convenient way of removing uninterested or ineffective people from the board. Such a matter must, of course, be handled with care, for some people have a dog-in-the-manger attitude about board membership or are offended if the unpalatable truth is suggested to them. The person or group who must make the decision at this point may decide simply not to reappoint or renominate a given member when his term has expired; in that case some appropriate (though not wholly truthful!) farewell ceremony or communication must be arranged. If the selecting authority feels that such an abrupt cut-off is not appropriate, he may want to talk to the errant member in some such vein as this: "Jim, your term will soon be up, and the nominating committee wants to know whether you want to accept an-

67

other appointment. We've noticed that you haven't been too active recently and wonder if you've lost interest. How about it?" The person thus addressed with greater or less subtlety, has two alternatives: to leave the board; or to accept another term with the resolution that he will mend his ways.

Unfortunately, the problem of rotation is not so easy as the foregoing paragraph has made it sound. Some people, even though they go on record as resolving to do better, do not actually do so. And the system does not work very well so far as earnest though ineffective members are concerned. Therefore, some authorities argue that a more automatic device must be found: limitation of the number of consecutive terms which a given member may have.

Before that device is discussed, however, it is appropriate to point out that definite terms sometimes create problems and hardships for a board. Perhaps the major difficulty is that effective and capable people, whose continuing membership is greatly needed, sometimes feel that they *should* leave the board at the end of a given term. Their minds cannot be changed, even by the most vehement assurances from everyone. Also, it is possible that in some cases long-range thinking and continuity are hampered by the establishment of terms.

Despite these occasional difficulties, authorities agree that most boards should have definite, overlapping terms of membership.

14. LIMITATIONS OF TENURE

No such agreement exists concerning the limitation of the number of terms which a board member may serve.

The idea itself is a fairly simple one: every member should be required to leave the board after he has served a consecutive number of terms, usually one, two, or three. This arrangement may be eased a bit by permitting someone who is serving as an officer to finish such service. Usually people who serve on the board and are "rotated" off will not be invited to rejoin, but people who are particularly outstanding might be re-elected after a lapse of time. Special provisions can be made to retain the interest of past board members by having them serve in some special voluntary, honorary, or advisory capacity.

The reasons for the adoption of this device have already been suggested. Its chief drawback lies in the fact that some boards apparently need members with long tenure. Also, of course, there is something rather arbitrary and mechanical about the limitation of service, implying as it does that boards need to be protected against their own members.

But the idea has impressive sponsorship among authorities on the various kinds of boards. Some states have laws which limit the tenure of those who serve on certain kinds of public boards. Nobody would argue that the device should be universally used, but it is fair to say that for most boards some kind of limitation of service should be seriously considered, particularly when the above-mentioned easements and safeguards are adopted.

15. OFFICERS

Boards need officers to carry out general co-ordinative functions and to undertake special assignments. Most boards have at least four such positions, though some have more. They are the chairman, the vice-chairman, the secretary, and the treasurer. The duties of the last three are so common and so well understood that they do not need to be described here, though their functions should be clearly stated in the constitution or by-laws. But the chairmanship is so significant as to deserve special attention.

It is the key position in the life of the board and in the success of the agency or association. Each new chairman should be chosen with great care, and the board must be constantly aware of the need to develop leaders who can eventually serve in the top post. The chairman bears the greatest responsibility of any individual connected with the agency; he must be able to rise to this responsibility and carry it out. He should be able to evoke co-operation from the board members. He should be able to work harmoniously with the executive. He should be an effective representative to the constituency and the outside publics. The desirable traits of an ideal board chairman are, indeed, almost infinite but, rather than make a longer list of them here, it will probably be better to let them be-

70

come explicit in terms of the requirements of an effective board as they are expressed throughout this book; for, in a very real sense, the chairman embodies and is responsible for the board. The other officers (with the possible exception of the vice-chairman) all have special functions; only the chairman must accept over-all controlling direction.

One important distinction should be made between associations and agencies so far as board chairmen are concerned. The chairman of the board of an association is a member of that association and, if it embodies a professional group, he is a member of the profession. Thus a lawyer would be head of a legal society, a doctor of a medical society, a union member of a union, and a Junior League member of the Junior League. In such situations, there would be no professional distinction between the backgrounds of the chairman (and other board members) and the executive and staff. In agencies, however, particularly those which carry out professionalized functions—such as welfare, health, education, or religion—the chairman is not and should not be a member of the profession concerned. (Many authorities would include *all* board members and not just the chairman and there is good ground for this contention.) A teacher should not be chairman of a school board, a minister should not be chairman of a church board, a librarian should not be chairman of a library board, and a doctor should not be chairman of the board of a hospital. The reason for this rule lies in the funda-

71

mental point made in Chapter One that a lay, volunteer, citizen board is usually delegated—formally or informally—by society to control the policies of a specialized professional agency. The chairman must symbolize the community, or at least the constituency, and not the profession. This distinction is not merely a theoretical one, as countless boards have discovered to their cost and sorrow, when the chairman and the executive have entered into conflict, or one of them has achieved an unhealthy dominance over the other.

Ideally there should always be several persons who would be competent enough to take over the chairmanship. One of the major tasks of each occupant of that post is to consider how he may develop the potential for leadership of each member so that either immediately or in subsequent years, the board will always have a supply of persons who are able to assume the major responsibility. He should also be concerned with establishing a smooth transition of his office into other hands and with avoiding any of the three main problems of choosing a new chairman with which boards are sometimes confronted.

Sometimes there are several actively competing candidates for the chairmanship, and each may have a faction supporting him. This situation arises most often perhaps on the boards of industrial and commercial corporations, but it is not uncommon elsewhere. In such a circumstance, an effort should be made by the present chairman or someone else to try to work out a compromise, such as the establishment of a line of succession so that the various strong candidates can take their turn. Occasionally, too, the matter of personalities can be translated into issues, so that the divisive questions can be solved. But such solutions are not always possible and, where the battle is joined, there is often no alternative but to let the matter be fought out and brought to a decision in the open. In such a case, it may be helpful to reflect, more or less philosophically, that a board is designed by its very nature to include people with different points of view and that the doctrine of majority rule is the best means yet found to resolve conflicts. But when the battle is over, and one side has won, it is important to patch up the wounds in any way possible, and to try to prevent a recurrence of the struggle.

Another problem which arises more frequently than it should is that sometimes there is nobody competent to succeed to the chairmanship. When this happens, it is always a commentary on previous chairmen that they have not sufficiently prepared the way for their own succession, but the assessing of blame does little good. What is to be done? There is no good way out of the situation, but one of at least three solutions is usually adopted. First, the ablest person available is selected and buttressed with as strong an executive committee and group of committee chairmen as is possible. Second, an ex-chairman of the board is persuaded to reassume the role for a while until a better line of succession can be found. Third, a new board member is found and immediately made chairman; obviously, if this choice is made, such a person should make up in general competence and personality what he lacks in specific knowledge.

Still another problem occurs when someone in whom the board has little confidence is directly in line of succession for the chairmanship. When this happens, the board must assess the possible damage of his selection and decide which is the lesser evil: rejecting him, or giving him the post. If it chooses the former course of action, it should do what it can to protect him against loss of face and hurt feelings. Also it should try to salvage his special talents and his support of the program. If it decides to appoint him, it may aid the situation by building an unusually strong executive committee. It may groom another candidate to succeed to his place as soon as possible. It may rely more heavily on committee decisions and take fewer matters to the whole board than is usually the case. And it may indicate informally to the executive that this is a time in which to exercise general caution.

All the foregoing observations imply that a chairman should not hold his post too long. Most of the considerations affecting tenure of board members which were mentioned earlier also apply to the officers of the board. The point to keep in mind is that each board must decide how long it is appropriate for one person to serve as chairman. If the tenure of each chairman is too short, the board and the agency or association are prevented from having the developed leadership which only responsible experience can bring. Particularly in boards concerned with complex programs, the chairman needs time to master the intricacies of board management and to reveal his own capacities. But the board also needs to have the continuity of active and vital leadership which, in most cases, cannot be achieved except by a periodic change of chairmen.

16. COMMITTEES

Of all aspects of board membership, the committee is the most subject to mock horror and heavyhanded humor. Each year seems to turn up a clever new definition of a committee which soon grows overfamiliar with use.[2] When a committee is appointed during a meeting of the board, those at whom the finger points affect a shudder of dismay. One eminent authority on boards has announced that to have one committee is better than to have two, to have two is better than to have three, and so on. It is all too clear what would be better than one committee.

Despite all this official and unofficial disapproval, committees continue to flourish, and there are very good reasons why they should. Before going into this matter, however, it is important to understand that there are at least three different kinds of board committees.

---

[2] For example: a committee is a group of people who keep minutes and waste hours; a committee is an organization of individuals who separately can do nothing, but who collectively can decide that nothing can be done.

The most prevalent and the most criticized are *standing committees,* which may be defined as those which remain in existence indefinitely in order to consider a certain category of problems or actions. Among standing committees which are frequently found are those which have to do with program, personnel policies, nominations, buildings and grounds, investment, and budget. Usually standing committees study problems in their assigned areas, provide specialized assistance and advice to the executive and staff, recommend policies for adoption by the board, and, occasionally, provide direct service.

Special committees are appointed to handle a particular situation or problem. They go out of existence when it has been dealt with. Such a committee might be appointed to screen applicants for the post of executive, to discuss a special situation or problem and bring back a recommendation to the board, to plan a special event, to represent the board in some conference or negotiation, or to carry out any of the myriad other responsibilities which seem to arise in the day-to-day life of any board.

Co-ordinative committees are those which provide general direction and guidance for the work of the board. The executive committee usually is the only example of this sort on most boards, although other co-ordinative committees are sometimes appointed when it is thought essential to bring together subgroups which are concerned with several particular functions. A finance committee, for example, may be composed of all those persons on the board who have responsibility for securing and handling funds. The executive committee is usually made up of the officers of the board and the chairmen of the major standing committees. Other people may also be added; frequently, for example, the immediate past president or the president-elect are included. The executive committee provides a relatively small group which can meet regularly or on call to deal with minor matters, make recommendations to the board on major issues, handle emergencies, make future plans, and appraise accomplishment.

Most of the values of committees have been implied in the foregoing discussion of their nature and functions, but it may be useful to provide a quick summary of the reasons why committees are often proposed or defended. They provide the opportunity to make special investigations and clarify policy; to use the special talents of board members; to carry out functions which are essential but which do not require the time of the full board; to aid in the involvement of members; to help train board members for positions of responsibility; to strengthen weak board officers; to speed up decisions; to permit the discussion of confidential matters not appropriate with a whole board; to give recognition to active board members; and to proclaim the board's interest in a certain subject or field of work.

Special committees are so clearly essential to the conduct of the business of most boards that little attack is made against them. With standing and co-ordinative committees, however, the reverse is the case. As was pointed out earlier, some authorities have a strong dislike for such committees, particularly in public boards and most especially in boards of education. A heavy onslaught is mounted against them, and some of the most telling weapons are the following arguments: Such committees weaken the whole board by usurping its power. They reduce effective participation or criticism by other board members. (In one school board, in five years, 214 out of 217 committee reports were adopted with no change.) They create overlapping jurisdictions. They cause delay and postponement of action. They take up too much time of board members. They create special interest groups who lose sight of the over-all integrative function of the board. Such committees turn into small boards for particular purposes. They lead committee members to believe that they are technical experts and encourage them to usurp executive and staff functions. By weakening the board as a whole, they keep the executive from having a central group with which to work. They also have a tendency to put the board members into direct contact with the staff, thereby weakening the executive's co-ordinative powers.

Amidst these gusts of dissenting opinion, we must turn to a familiar solution: each board should decide for itself how many and what kinds of committees it wants to have. The sharp arguments just summarized have been included as a way of helping any such board to make its own judgments more thoughtfully.

If a board does decide to have committees, it should resolve to have good ones. Most of the arguments against committees mentioned above are, in fact, arguments against bad committee practices. Board members have usually had a great deal of experience with committees in other connections and understand reasonably well the need for a committee to know what it is doing, to act as a true group and not fall subject to the domination of one member, to know its own limitations, and to pursue its activities with vigor. These fundamental matters, being common to all committees, will therefore not be dealt with here. There are, however, several points which relate particularly to standing and co-ordinative committees and which do deserve mention.

The size of the board is directly related to the need for committees. In a small board, it is wise for every member to participate in all activities so that he is fully involved in the total work, is well rounded in terms of his total knowledge of board activities, and is more effective in carrying out his duties. Larger boards, however, must usually set up more highly structured ways of achieving the board's purposes; and this fact almost inevitably leads to the appointment of committees.

Whenever a committee is appointed, its functions should be clearly stated *in writing*. Standing and co-ordinative committees are usually provided for in the by-laws and in such cases the functions should be included there. As with other provisions of the by-laws, there should be a periodic review of these statements of function to be sure that they are up to date. The functions of special committees should be recorded in the minutes at the time such committees are provided for or appointed.

A committee has only those powers which are delegated to it by the board and it should take only those actions which it knows have board approval. Ordinarily the board should approve in advance or ratify afterward all the actions and decisions of a committee. In emergency situations a committee (especially an executive committee) sometimes has to make a decision without consulting the whole board. In such a case it must ask itself what it thinks the whole board would support, if possible consulting with some of the other members individually to find their wishes. But emergencies should be treated as emergencies, and not give rise to established practices.

Committees are usually appointed by the chairman, often after consultation with the board and sometimes after ratification by it. (In some situations, there is even a "committee on committees.") The chairman is usually an *ex-officio* member of all committees, but if he chooses to exercise his option to participate, he must be careful not to dominate the committee or it will fail to achieve its most important functions. The executive should, in most cases, also have a right to sit with committees, though he

80

may not always wish to exercise that right. He should never participate in a committee's activities when it is considering some matter that has to do with his own qualifications or conditions of tenure.

The appointment of committees is one of the most interesting and creative jobs of the chairman. As he thinks about each particular assignment, he should hold two primary qualities in mind: competence and interest. He is fortunate if both these qualities coincide in a given individual. If they do not, he must either get the competent person interested or the interested person competent. This is not merely a play on words; it is part of the long process of training for leadership which all boards undertake by accident or by intention. If a desired committee member is competent but does not want to take on the task, the chairman must use his powers of persuasion. If a board member desires a post on a given committee (or, failing a desire, has even a readiness) but does not yet have adequate ability, the chairman must try to see that he gets the skill that he needs. In this latter connection, it is often helpful if a board chairman appoints as a member of each committee someone who has a good potentiality for becoming a future chairman of it.

Understandably enough, some people get stereotyped in their assignments. An investment counselor, for example, is so obvious a choice as chairman of the investment committee that he often has a permanent assignment to that post. Perhaps this is indeed the best way to use his talents, but it is well to remember that competent people are often competent in many things. Frequently, it is amazing to see with what fresh energy such a person will tackle a new task if given an opportunity to escape from the staleness of overfamiliar duty.

In some situations, board committees are supplemented by people chosen from outside the board. A university, for example, may have a number of standing committees, each devoted to some major division of the university's work. On each committee there may be a nucleus of board members supplemented by people drawn from the community. Such special assignments give the agency or association additional support, increase the representation involved, broaden the knowledge which can be brought to bear on the problem, provide the opportunity for good public relations, and offer a good point of recruitment for new board members. These values are achieved, of course, only when such committees operate vigorously and effectively.

If the board does not have any committees, it becomes in effect a committee of the whole and in this way can gain the values which good committee work provides. If there are committees, the chairman will usually find that no other part of his job is so important as their selection and stimulation. Just as an executive must work closely with his major staff members, so must the chairman of the board with his committee chairmen. To do so provides him with one of the most creative aspects of his job as he attempts to challenge, motivate, and blend the personalities of the board members into a cohesive, energetic, and effective whole.

17. AUXILIARY BOARDS

Many agencies have more than one board. In such a case, one board has ultimate legal power and responsibility and the other or others perform special services. Thus a welfare agency may have both a board and a women's board. (Sometimes, in this case, the first is called "the men's board," and many are the misunderstandings which have arisen from the use of that term!) The auxiliary boards are often differentiated by sex, age, or geography. A hospital, for example, might have a women's board, a young men's board, and several regional boards for various parts of the city. Each such board operates essentially like a controlling board in most of the matters with which this book deals. The values of a multiple-board arrangement may be simply stated: the agency is helped in various essential ways, usually money raising, public relations, and volunteer services; and a group of potential board members gains experience and demonstrates its competence.

But the headaches which can be created by a multiple-board system are both numerous and difficult to cure. An auxiliary board may gain a great deal of prominence and prestige, and be confused in the public mind—or, worse, in its own—with the board where the controlling power lies. An auxiliary board may gradually take on more and more functions until it exactly parallels the controlling board; in such a case, there is in effect a two-house legislature and every issue must be carried through both boards—to the eventual despair of the executive. Two boards may quarrel, or become deadlocked, or have any other kind of difficulties imaginable, all to the detriment of the service or program they are supposed to guide and aid.

The basic rule for preventing or curing these difficulties is this: auxiliary boards should be auxiliary. Only one board can be controlling. The others must have clear-cut functions which they carry out, and these functions should be set down in writing and generally understood. When an auxiliary board helps with a function, the controlling board is not relieved of responsibility by that fact. An auxiliary board, for example, may have money raising as its central purpose but, if it fails, the controlling board still must raise the money.

Some plan must also be worked out for co-ordinating activities, particularly when there are several auxiliary boards. One device is overlapping membership; often the president of each auxiliary, during his term as president, is a member of the controlling board. Another device is a co-ordinating committee of the chairmen and other central officers of each board. But no matter what formal devices are evolved, none can be a substitute for careful day-today planning to be sure that relationships remain smooth.

CONCLUSION

It is well to stress at the end, as at the beginning, the fact that boards are essentially human enterprises. They work much better if the people concerned know clearly what they are doing and are related effectively to one another. But structure provides merely the potentiality for action. Only as a board carries out its functions with vigor and imagination is it infused with life. As an eighteenth-century philosopher put it, "The flour is the important thing, not the mill. When we ask what time it is we don't want to know how watches are constructed."[3] And yet, you cannot have the flour without the mill, nor know the time without a watch.

---

[3] C. C. Lichtenberg, *Reflections*, 1799.

CHAPTER FOUR

The Board, the Executive,
and the Staff

WITHIN the sphere of freedom left to it by outside controls, the board[1] has unlimited interest and influence. It cannot mark out any one activity as its own special responsibility, nor can it permit itself to be denied authority over any such activity. Whatever is of concern to the agency or association must be of concern to the board, either actually or potentially.

The same principle is true of the executive. Individual members of the staff have special assignments, but the executive must be concerned with the total operation. Even when the board relieves him of responsibility for some particular function, he still

---

[1] In this chapter, except for Section 24, the word "board" will mean the board of an agency or association. Section 24 deals briefly with the special situation of auxiliary boards. Many of the comments made in the earlier sections do have some relevance for auxiliary boards.

has the obligation to consider it to be part of the whole program and to warn the board when he believes that the function is not being adequately performed.

The staff carries out the program. Each member has his own duties, but all the various special assignments must be brought together into a co-ordinated whole. The staff is responsible directly to the executive but ultimately to the board.

This chapter will explore the complicated relationship among these three vital parts of any agency or association, dwelling partly on structure but chiefly on operation.

18. JOINT RESPONSIBILITY

The relationship between the board and the executive is a partnership for which both are responsible. Like all such intimate human bonds, this one is filled with points of possible tension and difficulty. Just as nobody can write a prescription which would make all marriages happy, so no one can suggest a formula for a universally successful board-executive partnership. But its effectiveness can be greatly enhanced if its true nature is understood.

A first essential is to realize that it *is* a partnership. In most cases, the board is both legally and actually the dominant partner. It usually selects the executive, sets the conditions of his work, and, when it wishes, replaces him. This kind of ultimate authority has a profound influence. But the executive has

87

real authority, too. Sometimes it derives from his profession, sometimes from his prominence, and sometimes from his personality and ability. At the very minimum, he deserves the respect accorded to his position as head of the agency or association. The board must recognize this fact and operate always in terms of equality of approach. The arbitrary exercise of authority over its executive by a board should be considered a last resort, something like a declaration of war in the relations between nations.

The board-executive system of dual responsibility has its roots deep in American tradition, and its influence is spreading. Its values lie in the fact that it makes possible combinations of influences which, in some sense, run counter to one another but which are needed for effective results. To understand and to guide the board-executive relationship, one must understand how each of the two parties complements the other.

The board is corporate and acts only on the basis of group discussion and decision. The executive is individual and acts with the authority and integration of a single personality.

The board is continuous. The executive is temporary. This distinction is not always apparent, particularly where executives have had a long tenure and board members a short one. While its members may come and go, the board endures, and it has an obligation always to act in terms of a long-range perspective. The executive has the direct responsibilities of operation. He should carry them out with due regard to ultimate as well as immediate considerations, but he must always face the fact that he will not be present forever, whereas presumably the board will be.

The board is part-time. The executive is full-time. He is identified with the agency and typically earns his livelihood from it. His work is a central focus of his life. The board, though always in existence, can call only on the part-time services of its members.

The board has ultimate responsibility, subject to the requirements laid upon it by external authority. The executive, because he holds his office at the pleasure of the board, has a more limited responsibility.

One other comparison is more relevant to the boards of agencies than to the boards of associations. The board of an agency is typically made up of people who are lay and non-expert in the program, although they often possess special knowledge in matters which relate to its work; they represent the broad community or constituency. The executive is usually a professional or possessed of expert competence. He represents the agency itself and the profession or activity with which its program is concerned.

19. POLICY AND ITS EXECUTION

In so complex a relationship, many authorities on boards have sought a single, fundamental rule by which to define the function of the board as contrasted to the function of the executive. The mind, in its search for certainty, finds a powerful fascination in setting up some central concept and then trying to relate all experience to it. Usually, although not always, the rule suggested is that the board should determine policy and the executive should carry it out. This distinction is significant in political theory, particularly in the United States, and therefore it has often been used by those who have brought various kinds of boards under their observation. In the board-executive relationship it is easy to see an analogy with Congress and the President, with a legislature and a governor, and with a city council and a mayor.

Unfortunately, the effort to distinguish between a board and an executive in terms of this single rule runs into a significant difficulty: it is demonstrably not in accord with the facts. A whole school of writers has denied that the distinction is valid even in government, but, if it were, the analogy with politics still would not hold. The major distinctions between a board and its executive are those outlined in the previous section and are completely different from those which define the differences between Congress and the President. Moreover, boards must perform a number of executive and judicial functions, such as selecting an executive, carrying on financial campaigns, arbitrating serious conflicts within the staff, and performing volunteer services for the program. The executive, on the other hand, has an important role in policy making. When he takes fundamental

90

matters to his board for decision, he usually feels an obligation to recommend the course of action it should take. In this process, he guides the thought of the board. Furthermore, in the day-to-day operation of the agency or association, he makes a great deal of policy, and the total effect of these immediate decisions may be far greater than the broad policies which the board lays down.

But if this classical distinction between policy making and execution is not the sole test of the difference between the board and the executive, it is a useful principle to follow wherever possible in actual operation. Wherever it can, the board should try to stay at the level of generality and not specificity, to think of categories of problems rather than individual difficulties, to consider long-range developments, and to put the program in the larger perspective of the whole community. The executive, on the other hand, must recognize that his is the immediate responsibility, that he must administer each situation as it arises, and that he should press the importance of his own specialism. These distinctions arise, however, out of the differences between board and executive which were explored in the previous section. They do not spring from the application of an arbitrary single rule.

20. THE RESPONSIBILITIES OF THE BOARD

The central concern of every board and executive must be to achieve the objectives of the program.

91

These objectives are always specific, not only to the type of agency or association concerned, but also to its particular location. A school system is established to educate the children and adults of a community. A church provides religious experience for its congregation. A hospital cares for the sick members of the constituency it is established to serve. Every agency or association has both a general function and a particular orbit of work, and these two taken together define its objectives. It is successful to the extent that these objectives are achieved.

But the goals of a program cannot be reached if the board does not function properly. To return to a physiological parallel, the normal human body must perform certain functions: it must, for example, hear, see, smell, breathe, touch, think, propel itself, and digest. These functions do not establish the aims which guide human life, but such aims cannot be accomplished if the body does not operate effectively. So it is with agencies and associations. They may not survive if they do not function well.

One cannot establish a list of functions for an agency or association as easily as for the human body, partly because there has not been so much research about them and partly because the social sciences are not so exact as the natural sciences. Also every analyst of boards makes an interpretation which is influenced by his own viewpoint. The following list of sixteen functions is presented with the awareness that not everyone will agree that it is comprehensive or that it is organized in the best possible way. But it has grown from a synthesis of the literature and from discussions in which more than 700 board members have participated. These functions are here stated in terms of board responsibility but, in the discussion of each function, the role of the executive is suggested. In those cases in which another section of this book is essentially a discussion of a function, the reader is referred directly to that section.

First, the board should keep the over-all objectives of the program clearly in focus and satisfy itself that the goals of the particular parts of the work or units of the organization are in harmony with these broad objectives (see Section 26).

Second, the board should assure itself that changing conditions are adequately reflected in the program. It should see that continuous planning is carried on, providing vision and a balanced perspective. It should scrutinize all proposals for change in the light of its judgment as to the best long-range course of action. The executive has the obligation to see that the planning procedures are carried out. More than that, he should feel free to propose courses of action to the board or make any comments he wishes about proposals made by others. He must always realize, however, that the board is finally responsible for the decision.

Third, the board should select the executive (see Section 22).

Fourth, the board should accept the obligation of working effectively with the executive and, through him, with the staff (see Sections 21, 22, and 23).

Fifth, the board should assure itself that the work of the agency or association is effectively organized by the proper assignment of responsibilities to staff members and the co-ordination of these special responsibilities into a harmonious whole. An organizational pattern, at least of a large enterprise, is never a wholly logical and consistent framework. It is, in part, the result of tradition, personality, and varying conceptions of the importance of particular tasks. The executive has the immediate responsibility to see that the organization is soundly conceived and operated or to revise it so that it will be more effective. The board has the right to expect that it will be kept informed about the form of the organization and that it will approve any major changes in it.

Sixth, the board should assure itself that the executive discharges effectively those directing powers which lie particularly within his area of responsibility. Among these powers are the development of sound personnel procedures, both in recruitment and in establishment of optimum conditions of work; the creation of a broad base of participation in decision making among the staff; the resolution of conflicts; the establishment of effective control mechanisms (such as budgeting, accounting, and purchasing) in the work of the agency; and the effective use of physical resources. These aspects of administration are, like the development of sound organization, the immediate responsibility of the executive. It is, however, the ultimate responsibility of the board to see that they are performed effectively.

Seventh, the board should serve as arbiter in conflicts between staff members on appeal from the decision of the executive and in conflicts between the executive and the staff. The members of a board usually dislike the duty of being judges but, on occasion, they cannot escape it, particularly in large and complex enterprises. The executive should do all that he honorably can to keep the board from becoming a court of appeal by forestalling conflicts, trying to resolve them himself, or seeing that they are resolved within the staff. He cannot always do so.

Eighth, the board should establish such broad policies governing the program as may be necessary to cover continuing or recurrent situations in which uniformity of action is desirable. The board may not need to frame the policies it adopts; usually, indeed, the policies will be drafted by the executive for consideration, revision, and adoption by the board. Furthermore, once the policies are adopted, either the executive or the board itself may suggest changes at any time. It is the duty of the executive to administer the program in terms of these policies, to understand the degree of latitude which is allowed to him in making exceptions in particular cases, to know when a policy applies and when it does not, and to deal with situations not covered by policy.

Ninth, the board should use the special knowledge and contacts of the individual board members in the improvement of the program. Board members perform countless minor services for the agency or association, and it is expected that they will do so. They should be certain that these services are appropriate and desired by both board and executive, since a well-meaning but unwelcome service can create more difficulties than it prevents or eases. When a board member undertakes a major direct service, he must be particularly sure that in becoming almost a staff member himself, he does not create problems for the executive. Also, both the board and the executive must be careful not to exploit the professional specializations of board members and ask them to undertake services which it is not appropriate for them to perform without compensation.

Tenth, the board should assure itself that the agency or association is effectively integrated with its environment and with the other organizations and publics to which it is related (see Section 30).

Eleventh, the board should accept responsibility for securing adequate financial resources. In the performance of this function, the board and the executive must collaborate closely, with the board taking an active part. The executive may, on occasion, do whatever is necessary to secure financial support himself, but ordinarily he acts with the board and often he serves merely as its agent.

Twelfth, the board should assure itself that its basic

legal and moral responsibilities are fulfilled. The executive should keep the board informed as to what he regards these responsibilities to be.

Thirteenth, the board should develop and abide by rules and procedures governing its own affairs. It and it alone can determine how its structure and operations are to be organized. The executive may make suggestions to the board in this respect, but he ought to do no more than that.

Fourteenth, the board should give to the agency or association the full support, prestige, and leadership of the board itself and of its individual members (see Section 7).

Fifteenth, the board should do everything in its power to keep its own membership able, broadly representative, and active (see Chapter Two).

Sixteenth, and finally, the board should appraise the program periodically to assure itself that the objectives are being achieved; if they are not, then either the objectives themselves or the means of achieving them must be revised. The executive ordinarily must collect the evidence on which the appraisal is based. Furthermore, he has the obligation to present all the findings to the board, the bad as well as the good. The board must know the truth about the program in order to know how to improve it.

21. THE BOARD AND THE EXECUTIVE

These functions cannot be carried out effectively unless both the board and the executive are capable and can work together. Curiously enough, some people have the idea that the board-executive system is merely a safeguard against the weakness of one or the other of the two parties. They argue: if you have a strong board, you don't need a strong executive, and if you have a strong executive, you don't need a strong board. This "seesaw" principle may be true for short periods of time, but in the long run it is fatal to sound operation. A program flourishes only when it is conducted by both an effective board and an effective executive—and when both are able to work together.

This last point must be emphasized, because common observation reveals all too clearly that people involved in close human relationships do not always agree, and the stronger they are, the sharper may be their conflict. The board-executive relationship, since it is necessarily so close, can never be completely free of sources of tension. The result, at least occasionally, may range from irritation to open conflict. Many an executive has felt about a board the way the Quaker spinster did about a husband: it takes a very good one to be better than none. Sometimes boards have also the same feeling about their executives.

The only sensible rule in any particular situation is to mark out as clearly as possible the particular responsibilities of the board and of the executive, using the distinctions made in the last two sections of this book. A shadowy zone of accommodation will still remain. Just as a husband and a wife, a parent and a child, or two business partners must learn to adjust to one another, so must a board and its executive. When sparks begin to fly within the zone of accommodation, the point of tension should be faced, discussed, and, if possible, settled before it and its consequences have grown too great.

The executive tends to be the chief architect of the relationship between himself and the board. He always has certain advantages in that relationship, since he is on the job full time, he is an expert, the work of the agency is his central concern, and he often has a lengthy tenure. Also, the relationship is more sharply significant to him than it is to any member of the board.

In their depth of interest and excess of zeal, executives sometimes go about the task of building the relationship in the wrong way. Miss Florence Nightingale provides us with a good example. Her first position was as superintendent of the Institution for the Care of Sick Gentlewomen in Distressed Circumstances. About this experience, she wrote ruefully:

> When I entered "into service" here, I determined that, happen what would, I NEVER would intrigue among the Committee. Now I perceive that I do all my business by intrigue. I propose, in private, to A, B, or C, the resolution I think A, B, or C most capable of carrying in Committee, and then leave it to them, and I always win.[2]

---

[2] Quoted in: Cecil Woodham-Smith, *Florence Nightingale, 1820-1910* (New York: McGraw-Hill Book Co., Inc., 1951), p. 76.

Probably no executive in the world has ever failed to do at least a little of the intriguing of which Miss Nightingale accused herself, and perhaps some of it is occasionally essential. But, as the wryness of her remark reveals, she recognized the error of this procedure. Carried very far, it means that the executive dominates the board, a situation which is about as likely to give trouble as when the board dominates the executive!

The executive has the right to expect that the chairman will take the initiative in mobilizing board activities. If the chairman does so, there is no problem. If he does not, the proper course for the executive is to suggest to him, as deftly and as positively as possible, where his responsibilities lie.

The chairman, in turn, has a right to expect that the executive will accept full partnership with the board. Occasionally an executive, because of long tenure, commanding personality, or extraordinary competence, dominates the board, even while ostensibly observing all the forms of deliberation and permitting the board to decide on small matters. When this happens, the chairman has the responsibility to regain as much of the lost control for his board as he possibly can, acting with such tact and concern for the proprieties as he can muster.

Where the board—or its chairman—exerts a dominant role, reducing its executive to little more than a clerk, the remedy is often not very clear. Usually such a board cannot get an executive who is capable of acting as a real partner and therefore the situation is perpetuated. In such cases, the remedy may have to be applied from outside by the appointing or electing authority. For example, a group of citizens may mobilize to secure a better school system and, in the process, elect a new school board which is committed to bringing in and working with a strong, professional superintendent.

In any case, it must be recognized that the relationship between board and executive is a subtle one, usually built up over a long time. Every board follows procedures which were established before the tenure of the present members, and every executive is haunted by the ghosts of his predecessors. Usually it takes time to bring about any fundamental change in the relationship. The process of change is typically one of evolution, not revolution.

22. THE BEGINNING, MIDDLE, AND END OF THE BOARD-EXECUTIVE RELATIONSHIP

To appoint and to uphold the executive are two of the most important functions of a board. The importance of his work, the intimacy of his relationship to the board, and the influence he has on the total program all require that the board exercise the greatest care in choosing the right person, in introducing him properly, in evaluating his work and helping him to improve, in honoring him on his retirement, and, if he does not prove satisfactory, in ending his employment.

Some boards think far ahead on the matter of the line of succession so that there is a clear and smooth transition from one executive to the next. Such a policy is sound if it does not lead to stagnation of policy or administration. Many boards, however, must take the selection of a new executive as a separate special problem and, if so, certain steps and policies are usually followed.

First, it is best if the task of finding a new executive can be carried out without haste and preferably with the opportunity to maintain continuity of direction of the program, so that there is a smooth transfer of duties from the old executive to the new one.

Second, the whole board should discuss the special criteria it wishes to establish for the new executive. Such a discussion may go off into a pointless cataloguing of virtues, but usually it is helpful in clarifying the minds of the board members about what kind of person they are seeking. This fact is particularly true if the qualities named are not merely generalized statements of what is needed by any executive, but are stated in terms of both the short-term and the long-term requirements of the particular agency or association. Often the criteria are determined in part by professional standards, and the board should be mindful of them. Many of the books in the Bibliography have useful suggestions about what points various kinds of boards should keep in mind. The board may wish, also, to have a memo-

randum from the present executive suggesting criteria, but its own discussion will be much freer if he
is not present.

Third, the board should invite the staff to share
in the task of selecting the executive. The necessity
for this step varies from one kind of agency to another, but it should be taken wherever possible. The
board needs to know the judgment of the staff concerning the major current problems of the agency and
the type of executive leadership needed at the present stage of development. The staff may also be able
to suggest possible candidates of requisite stature and
give its judgment concerning those candidates who
are nominated by other sources. Often the staff is
asked to elect a committee which meets jointly with
the board committee or has consultations with it.

Fourth, the board turns over the duties of selection
to a special committee, which goes through all the
following procedures: building up a list of prospective candidates, finding out whether they are available, collecting information about those who are, and
gradually weeding out from the list those persons who
appear not to be suitable for the post. If there are
auxiliary boards, the selection committee should consult with them. One special problem which often
arises is whether the executive shall be sought within
the present staff or from outside it. The committee
(and eventually the whole board) must consider this
point not in the abstract, but in terms of what candidates are available, and must make the final selection

in terms of its judgment about the proper balancing of various factors: the caliber of the candidates, staff morale, and the need for a fresh point of view in the program.

Fifth, the board considers the names of those persons whom the committee believes to be best suited to the position. The board may wish to interview all the candidates or it may delegate this interviewing to the committee. As for the final selection, every member of the board should share in the making of the decision. The executive has the right to know if he was the unanimous choice of the whole group or, if he was not, what reservations some of the board members may have had about him. Such factors are relevant to his own decision as to whether or not to accept.

In offering the post to the executive, the board should be clear-cut about the conditions of his employment—salary, term of office, responsibilities, authority, "fringe" benefits, and special conditions of work. Usually it is helpful to have all such matters in writing and made a part of the official record of the board. The executive also has the right to expect that the board will be honest with him about present conditions in the agency or association. He will usually ask searching questions before he accepts the position and he should be given honest answers. If the board feels that there are special problems which he will encounter, it should tell him about them. An executive who, on taking his post, discovers that he has been misled or misinformed or left in ignorance has proper cause for resenting his treatment by the board—and resentment provides a poor basis for co-operation.

Once the new executive has been appointed, the board must be sure that he is inducted properly. His selection may have created special problems of relationship with others who were not chosen and, if the board can do so, it should ease this situation. It should see that he meets the people of the community or the constituency and has a special introduction to those persons with whom he needs to work closely. It should help him and his family to make an effective social adjustment to his new position. Most of all, it should help to create a situation in which he can demonstrate his abilities. The board must be careful to withhold any negative verdict until the new executive has had a real chance to succeed. The new leader always faces many problems, and he should not be expected to work miracles—at least not immediately.

Of course, every board does begin to evaluate its executive almost at once, and it does so constantly thereafter. Through its consideration of his proposals, it gives or withholds its approval of his actions. In informal personal conversations, board members make comments and judgments about him. Usually a formal evaluation of his work occurs only when there is some crisis in his relationship with the board, and by that time it is often too late for him to be helped. It is a pity that systematic evaluations of executives are not more common, and, at least in theory, it would be quite possible to set up routine procedures for carrying them out. In practice, however, the matter is almost always left to the skill and tact of the chairman. He may find it possible to convey his own appraisal and what he believes to be that of the majority of the board. Sometimes, also, the executive helps the situation by asking periodically for an evaluation of his work.

If a board member has some serious complaint to make about the executive, the proper course is to make it to the chairman, not to the executive himself, not to the other board members, and certainly not to the public. Depending on the particular situation, the chairman may then either quiet the criticism himself, ask the executive for an accounting, or arrange for a discussion of the matter with the interested parties. In most cases, frank discussion will clear up a difficulty which otherwise would fester in secret.

In any vital board-executive relationship, there will be times when the board is divided on an issue of policy or procedure and when the executive must adopt some course of action to cope with this division. In a thoughtful article concerning school boards, Luvern L. Cunningham has analyzed seven defensible courses of action which the executive may follow. Of these, he concludes that the best is for the executive to try "to expand the levels of information, the range of alternatives and conceptions of the problem" so that ultimately the factions are not aligned against each other but against the problem.[3]

The difficulty is more acute when the board is split on factional lines and most serious of all when the chairman is himself a member of one of the factions. In such a case, the executive has a difficult role to play as he tries to bridge the gap—and often the widening gap—between those who should be united in his support. Sometimes such factionalism can be cured only from the outside by the selection of a new board. The executive must make the choice between whether he wishes to remain and try to hold things together or whether he must leave. His choice will depend in some measure on whether he is himself the issue in the factionalism.

Sometimes boards must come to the conclusion that the executive is not satisfactory and should be replaced. This decision should not be reached lightly, but the board should guard itself equally against rash action and against sentimentalism or timidity. Once the decision to remove the executive is made, the board should proceed with due regard to protecting the rights of the executive as an individual. If he is to be dismissed at the end of his contract period, he must be given a suitable advance notice. If his contract is to be broken, he should be given an adequate settlement. Even if he serves at the pleasure of the board without a formal contract, he should be given

[3] Luvern L. Cunningham, "The Superintendent and a Divided Board," *The School Executive*, LXXIX, No. 3 (November, 1959). 61.

full consideration; if appropriate, the board should give him some kind of severance pay.

The unpleasant job of informing the executive of the board's decision falls to the chairman, who may, if he wishes, ask one or two other members to share the duty with him. The executive should be given the opportunity to respond to the charges against him and to discuss the situation fully. If he cannot convince the board, he will very often resign, and usually should be given the opportunity to do so unless he has been guilty of some gross offense. If he chooses to fight his dismissal by going to the community or the constituency, the board must be resolute. As Sorenson observes in this connection, "Some fever inevitably accompanies an operation, but after the fever subsides, the patient feels better than before the surgery."[4] Once an executive knows that he is being discharged, it is probably best if he leaves as soon as possible; his continued presence is hard for him, for the board, and for the program.

Most executives bring their tenure to an end by either retiring or resigning to accept another post. The board has an obligation to carry out the appropriate ceremonies on either occasion, remembering that the administration of the program has been a central concern of the executive, often for many years, and that departure is a shock for him, particularly if he is retiring. The board must be unusually careful

---

[4] Roy Sorenson, *The Art of Board Membership* (New York: Association Press, 1950), p. 39.

108

to avoid negligence or a perfunctory approach to this matter. Many former executives have had their memory of their whole service soured by what they felt to have been casual or ungrateful treatment by their boards at the time of retirement. After all, the board-executive relationship is an intimate one, and should be brought to a close with the due regard which should be given to the ending of any profound human relationship.

23. THE BOARD AND THE STAFF

The board should extend to the executive a great deal of latitude so far as staff administration is concerned. As already noted, the internal organization should be clear to the board, which should approve any major structural changes. Also, the board usually needs to establish over-all personnel policies for the agency, dealing with such matters as recruitment, methods of appointment, salary classifications, special benefits, conditions and hours of work, retirement, and pensions. Once these matters have been settled at a policy level, the executive of the agency should be given a free hand, subject to such rights of appeal to the board as the personnel policy statement itself has provided.

There has been much disagreement concerning the rights of the board so far as appointment or promotion of staff members is concerned. A good case can be made for keeping the board entirely out of such matters. If the executive is to have responsibility, he must have authority. To hamper his right to select his staff would not only restrict his freedom of choice but would give staff members the feeling that they are responsible not to him but to the board. Moreover, boards have neither the time nor the competence to recruit candidates, to interview all applicants, to sift the evidence, and to decide whom to appoint. Such a task is clearly administrative, and therefore more appropriate for the executive than for the board. If the executive does carry out the task and merely presents the preferred name to the board, its approval is usually a formality without meaning.

On the other hand, there are dangers in giving the executive complete control. The board loses contact with the realities of the work when it does not decide upon the people who are to carry it out. When the executive leaves, the board may find that it has a group of people with whom it must work but for whom it feels no sense of responsibility. When a new executive is needed, the board may be confronted with the necessity for choosing the second-in-command (whom it did not select in the first place) or, if it refuses to do so, of creating a difficult personnel problem.

Here, clearly, is an area in which the board and the executive must collaborate, each one carrying out his appropriate responsibility in terms of the immediate situation. For one thing, the extent of the board's participation in staff appointments will vary according to the size of the agency or association; when there are large numbers of staff members, almost all authority must rest with the executive because the sheer weight of numbers makes active board participation impossible. Also, external factors often limit the freedom of choice. In public agencies, a civil service unit may control policies and, in many other cases, professional certification requirements sharply restrict the number of applicants. Operating within these limitations, perhaps the best policy is to divide the staff into three groups.

The first group consists of routine workers and people who are not professional or to whom the agency or association does not need to feel any permanent continuing responsibility. These persons should be selected by the executive or other administrative officers.

The second group consists of those people who hold substantial appointments or who are professional workers. In the case of institutions which confer permanent tenure after a period of probation, all persons recommended for such tenure should be included in this group. The executive here should make an initial selection of the persons (undertaking the necessary screening process), but the final appointment should be made by the board. If a member of the board knows any relevant facts about the person to be appointed, they can then be brought to the attention of the executive and the other board members. If there is anything unusual about any appointment, the executive can make it known, so that the

111

board acts with full knowledge. The executive is protected against a later charge that the board did not know the full situation and, in case of any difficulty as a result of unusual conditions, the board will feel some sense of responsibility. Occasionally when a name is presented, the board has a serious question as to whether it should give its approval. In such a situation, the case must be worked out on its merits by the board and the executive.

The third group consists of all those persons who are in direct line of succession to the position as executive. In filling such posts, the board should participate fully in the selection and appointment procedures, even, on occasion, to the extent of helping to screen applicants. The continuity of the board requires that it be directly involved in any appointment which may limit its future control over the selection of an executive.

In some kinds of agencies and associations, the staff collectively (or certain parts of it) has its own system of authority which operates outside the normal lines of administration. The faculty of a college or university has traditional and carefully guarded rights which are usually carried out through a formal structure of councils and committees. The medical staff of a hospital may be separately organized as a group. In other situations, unions or staff associations may have great authority. In each of such cases, the board must understand clearly the special conditions which limit its own authority and that of the executive.

112

Sometimes a special relationship exists between a member of the board and a member of the staff, springing from kinship, previous friendship, outside connections, or close collaboration in the work of the agency or association. Those who share in such a relationship are ethically bound to remember that the executive must retain over-all administrative responsibility for the whole program including supervisory powers over all staff members. Under normal circumstances, no board member, not even the chairman, has the authority to issue orders to a staff member except at the will of the board and then only through the executive or with his consent. The staff member, in turn, must not circumvent the authority of the executive by going to a board member with a complaint or trying to persuade him to be a special pleader for some aspect of the program. When these rules are broken, it is a clear sign that the board-executive relationship is in danger—or that it soon will be. As one library board member observed: "I don't know any more potent chemical in making the milk of human kindness turn sour than to have an assistant go to the board of trustees with complaints which should properly be made only to the head librarian."[5]

24. THE RELATIONSHIPS OF THE AUXILIARY BOARD

The relationship of an auxiliary board to the executive and staff is usually easier to understand (though

---

[5] F. A. Begole, "Why I Am a Trustee," *Public Libraries*, XXVI (May, 1921), 236.

not always to work out) than that of a controlling or associational board. An auxiliary board should have clear-cut functions which are defined and limited. It is therefore possible to think through relationships and establish them on a more definite basis than is possible with a board which is responsible for everything. Both the chairman of the controlling board and the executive will ordinarily need to work closely with the auxiliary board to be certain that it is carrying out its appropriate functions in a suitable fashion and that it is adequately related to the staff members who may be especially charged with those functions. Thus an auxiliary board of a welfare agency, in carrying out its responsibility to raise funds, may sponsor an annual benefit. In doing so, it will need the backing of the controlling board, the co-ordinative and stimulative assistance of the executive, and the special help of the public relations staff members.

CONCLUSION

Since this is a book about boards, the emphasis in this chapter has been on their part in the complex relationship with executives and staffs. But the focus might equally well have been on either of the other two. In fact, there are many more books about them than about boards.

The major point to remember is that all three are essential and all must know how to blend their efforts. They are not merely the three pieces of a puzzle to be put together in a certain way. A more appropriate

114

analogy would be to a chamber music trio in which each instrument combines with the others to make up a continuing whole. Each one shifts and changes with the themes and variations of a particular composition, but each obeys the rules set by its own nature and conforms to the dictates of the trio form. The only difference is that in the board-executive-staff relationship, there is no score to follow. Everything—harmony or discord—flows from the players themselves.

CHAPTER FIVE

Improving the Operation

of the Board

STRICTLY speaking, a board exists only when it is meeting, but everyone knows that in fact, it has a continuous life. Its most impressive moments usually come during its sessions, when it is shaping policy, but what goes on between sessions is also vital, in the guidance and service it gives and in the less tangible but important support which its very existence provides for the program. Its effect comes both from what it does and from what it is.

Like any other group of human beings, a board always takes on a distinctive social character which results from the way its members react to one another and to their environment. A board has traditions and habits, prevailing opinions and dissenting views, and a general spirit which ranges somewhere between daring and conservatism. The board usually has more significance for its members than they realize until

116

it is in some way threatened or forced into a situation in which its nature is radically changed, as when it merges with another board.

As function and operation are dealt with in this chapter, the reader should think of a board not in a narrow, wooden sense, full of formality and protocol, but as a dynamic social unity, always complex and often contradictory.

25. ACHIEVING AN EFFECTIVE GROUP SPIRIT

When a board is first created, it has no group spirit. It is merely a collection of individuals seated around a table with no sense of unity to draw them together; indeed they often eye one another with a certain amount of reserve or even suspicion. But as time goes on, a change occurs. Out of the interaction of personalities, there grows an intangible and indefinable sense of the uniqueness of this particular board.

This spirit defines the way in which the individual feels about the group and how he relates himself to it. If he belongs to several boards, he will even adjust his way of reacting, sometimes very markedly, as he moves from one to another. The social climate of one board may make him co-operative; that of another, apathetic; and that of a third, quarrelsome. This reaction is not merely his alone, although, to be sure, his particular personality is important in creating the total mood. Each of the three boards may have a comparable effect on their other members as well. How this happens nobody quite understands, for group spirit is like electricity. It cannot be seen or completely explained, but it can certainly be felt.

An effective group spirit on a board is one which attracts its members, makes them want to work with one another, and gives them a sense of pride and satisfaction in the program and the board itself. Such a spirit is a result of many causes, among which some of the most important are these: a strong belief in the program; a sense of progress in accomplishing its goals; a conviction of the worth and importance of the board itself, particularly in the eyes of the community; and a good personal relationship and interaction among the members. Any board which has all four is fortunate; it is also rare.

Let us see how these factors operate in a particular case, taking, as an example, a private child care agency which tries to help those unfortunate children who are in desperate circumstances and who have no families or friends to help them. Here, certainly, is a worthy cause, one which is easy to understand and which demands a response from all but the hard-hearted. This particular agency can serve about five hundred children a year and, since it gives individual attention to each one, progress in solving each child's difficulties can be measured with some degree of adequacy. Since this is an old and good agency, with endowment and community support and a highly professional staff, most children are helped effectively. The board itself has great prestige in the community and has had it for generations; some of its members are children or even grandchildren of earlier members. To have achieved a place on this board is evidence not only of social position but also of dedication to the work of the agency beyond any perfunctory lip service. It is impossible either to inherit or to buy membership. Moreover, for years the board has rejoiced in a succession of excellent chairmen, men and women who thought about the long-range development of both the agency and the board, who made certain that good people were chosen as members, that they were properly introduced to its work and to one another, that there was a succession of responsibilities for each member so that he grew in knowledge and responsibility, and that the board was organized and operated smoothly. The spirit of this board is so powerful that it can do almost anything it wants, it holds an important place in the lives of its members, and it sets a shining standard for the community.

Such a board may be rare—but only because there are, in American life, so very many boards. Actually, in almost every community, there is at least one board which approaches, if it does not reach, the high standard set by this example. All such boards suggest that an effective group spirit is a by-product of everything a board has done to improve itself, for all such actions lead to a stronger board, and therefore one in which its members may take a proper pride. Every section of this book is, in some sense, concerned with the improvement of group spirit.

119

But any board's morale may also be improved directly, by paying attention to the relationships among the members. Some people seem to understand almost intuitively the ways to build a strong group. Others have arrived at the knowledge through long experience and reflection. Still others are able to short-cut experience by studying the essential principles of good group process which have grown out of the research carried out during the past twenty-five years by psychologists and sociologists.[1]

Some of the qualities present in boards which have an effective group spirit are these:

(*a*) Every board member accepts every other board member with a due appreciation of his strengths and a tolerance of his quirks and weaknesses.

(*b*) There is an easy familiarity of approach among the members of the board with an awareness of one another's backgrounds and viewpoints.

(*c*) Everyone concerned with a particular decision actually helps to make it.

(*d*) The contribution of each person or group is recognized.

(*e*) The board has a sense of being rooted in some important tradition and of providing continuity for a program which has been and continues to be of importance.

(*f*) The whole attitude of the board is forward-look-

---

[1] For a brief and readable introduction to this research, see: Malcolm and Hulda Knowles, *Introduction to Group Dynamics* (New York: Association Press, 1959).

ing, and there is a confident expectation of growth and development in the program.

(g) There is a clear definition of responsibilities so that each person knows what is expected of him.

(h) The members of the board can communicate easily with one another.

(i) There is a sense that the whole board is more important than any of its parts.

(j) There is a capacity to resolve dissent and discord or, if it cannot be resolved, to keep it in perspective in terms of larger purposes.

(k) There is acceptance of and conformity to a code of behavior, usually involving courtesy, self-discipline, and responsibility.

(l) There is an awareness of the fact that all boards contain clusters or pairs of persons who tend to like or dislike one another, as well as some who may not be closely involved with others; but there is also a capacity to use these personal relationships as effectively as possible to achieve the larger purposes of the program.

(m) There is an ability to recognize and use the informal authority of individual board members which arises not out of their specific assignments on the board but their power, connections, wealth, age, or ability.

(n) In case of internal conflict, the group has the capacity to examine the situation objectively, identify the sources of difficulty, and remedy them.

(o) Most important of all, the board members share

121

a clear understanding of and commitment to the cause which the agency serves.

To recognize such aspects of an effective group spirit as these is to take the first step toward their achievement. Once again we must assign to the chairman of the board a chief responsibility, but the task of building morale must be shared by all the members. To anyone who feels that the group spirit of a particular board should be strengthened, it will be useful to go over the list of fifteen aspects just mentioned. If he sees that his own board is failing in some respect, he may then use his ingenuity to see what can be done to remedy the situation.

All these qualities demand both constant effort and a considerable degree of subtlety, but some of them are easier to accomplish than others. If a board is stiff and formal, there are some fairly obvious ways to help it relax and gain an easier familiarity of approach, though the problem may need to be tackled not at the board meeting itself but in outside informal contacts. Giving suitable recognition for accomplishment is also fairly easy, although it is surprising how often its importance is forgotten.

Helping members to be able to communicate with one another is somewhat more difficult. To achieve this goal it may be necessary to help committees know how to put their special reports in such a form as to be readily understood by the other members. Also, senior members of a board may have a ready famili-

122

arity with special terms and processes; they can speak easily to one another out of their shared experience, but the newer members may not understand them. In such a case, it is a service to the group to ask clarifying questions. People sometimes hesitate to do so for fear that they will be thought stupid, but, as was pointed out in Chapter Two, it is surprising how often a hesitantly voiced desire to have things explained strikes a strong responsive chord among the rest of the board.

Perhaps the hardest of all group attributes to achieve are the most general—and the most obvious. To get all board members to accept one another with appreciation and tolerance would seem to be an evident need of every board and one which is almost a first requisite of success. In practice, however, such a situation is often very difficult to achieve and to maintain, particularly on a board which has representation from a number of different kinds of groups. All the tensions and problems of the community or constituency are present on the board in miniature and are just as likely to be accentuated as to be relaxed by the intimacy of the board situation. To achieve acceptance and tolerance is never easy and sometimes impossible. But anyone on the board can try to serve as interpreter between two antagonistic board members, to enlarge whatever area of agreement *is* possible, to serve as a continuing example of the tolerant and accepting approach himself, and, if possible, to bring the opposing members into some kind of situation, either inside or outside the board, in which they can work together and through shared common effort, build up the bonds of association.

26. THE DEFINITION OF OBJECTIVES

The objectives of an agency or association establish the basic framework of purpose which guides its program. If the board does not have a clear idea of objectives, then none of its actions can ever be quite right.

To illustrate this point, let us consider a museum. Such an institution often has four major purposes: to display the treasures it possesses; to educate the general public; to carry on research; and to train specialists in the subject matter field of the museum. These objectives influence everything about the museum, including the budget, the kinds of staff members engaged, the allocation of space, the nature of the displays, and the efforts to have good public relations. Suppose, however, that in a given museum there is no clear, balanced statement to guide and co-ordinate the activities of the board, the executive, and the staff. In such a situation the board is never quite clear what the objectives are. Some members will assume that one kind of activity is important, and others will espouse another. Some will want to carry on traditions, and others will want to follow what they regard as pioneering practices. Some may not realize that it is appropriate for a museum to have more than one purpose, and some may never think of purpose at all but

124

merely take the program for granted as having some internal logic of its own.

This sort of situation exists rather oftener than is sometimes realized. It is surprising that this fact is true because, though people join boards for many reasons, perhaps the most powerful one is that they believe in the purpose of the agency or association. But this belief may be more emotional than rational. A man who has children may feel a concern about their education and therefore accept nomination to the school board. A woman whose husband has died of a disease may join the board of a local association whose purpose is to combat that disease. Such deeply felt motivations as these may be accompanied by an equal depth of understanding of the programs concerned, but often they are not. Indeed, the very ardor of the new board member may lead him to fix on some one goal of an agency and drive toward it, with the result that the accomplishment of other goals suffers.

Objectives are of two major sorts. The first kind are general statements of purpose, spelled out sufficiently clearly so that they may be understood. The four museum objectives mentioned above are of this sort. The second kind of objectives are more specific; they define particular program emphases or goals, often for an established period of time. Usually they are directly related to the general goals. The board of the museum, for example, may set as its specific goals for a given year: to improve the collection by adding at least one major acquisition; to sponsor three special displays built around important themes; to find the funds to add another full-time research worker to the staff; and to try to recruit a larger number of able young people as students in the museum school.

These illustrations demonstrate an important point: both general and specific objectives are concerned with the program of the agency or association and not merely with the board itself. Boards may actually set specific targets for themselves—to broaden the representativeness of membership, to raise more funds, to write a set of by-laws, or to review the personnel policies—but these are always subordinate to the objectives of the agency or association. A board never exists for itself alone, nor for any special separate purpose of its own; if it acts as though it did, it is almost certain to get into trouble itself and the program will almost surely suffer.

In some kinds of agencies or associations, the nature of the objectives and of the resulting program is broadly understood. The definition of purpose is largely a matter of setting down the basic goals so that they are clear, particularly as they apply to the specific agency or association concerned. Thus, although the functions of hospitals are widely understood and are generally the same, each specific hospital has its own framework of purpose.

In other situations, the objectives may not be clearly understood and may, in fact, be hard to state exactly. Settlement houses, for example, often have difficulty in making the purposes of their programs clear, partly because they are so general in their service, partly because they have changed their functions and services rather markedly in the past fifty years, and partly because the recreational and informal educational activities, although the visible parts of the settlement's program, are not the ends but the means through which the professional worker tries to help people achieve certain social goals. In all such cases, the executive and the staff have an unusually heavy responsibility to interpret purposes, particularly to the board itself.

Whether understanding of objectives comes easily or with great difficulty, the board must be aware of them. Practically speaking, as has already been pointed out, there is no other way of gaining the proper perspective. In this connection, three major endeavors are essential.

First, every board should adopt a statement of the general objectives of the agency or association. Sometimes these are included in the constitution or by-laws but, if they are, they are often worded in such general terms as not to give much useful guidance. The board, however, must operate with more exact purposes. The first draft of any statement of general objectives should come from the executive and staff. It should then be studied and discussed by the entire board, every member of which should be involved in the process. A special committee may also be ap-

127

pointed to give the statement particular scrutiny. After full discussion and deliberation, the objectives should be endorsed by the board.

Second, the general objectives should be formally reviewed by the board at least once a year. No program can endure without making countless shifts to accommodate itself to the changing social conditions in which it operates. Also there may be advances in the field of work which have profound implications. (Orphans used to be put into asylums; now they are placed in foster homes. Medical advances have radically changed the character of many kinds of specialized hospitals.) The board should never be perfunctory in making its annual review of objectives. The executive and the staff should provide specialized guidance but the whole board should give the matter its attention. If major shifts in policy appear desirable, some special committee work may also be useful.

Third, specific objectives should be established periodically. Boards are greatly helped by setting goals for themselves. To work indefinitely toward general objectives is not enough. Demonstrations of concrete accomplishment are much more likely to occur if they are deliberately planned. When a board has accepted a particular goal and has set itself a deadline, there is a focusing of effort which cannot be achieved in any other way. Specific objectives may become part of the annual program or budgetary review, but should not be so submerged in other matters as to obscure the fact that the board is setting goals for itself and for the program.

Some boards, while accepting the necessity for having clear objectives, prefer to define them in a more informal fashion than is suggested here, letting questions of broad purposes or specific goals arise as they appear naturally in the course of the board's work. Such a policy may be used in very complex agencies or associations, in those which have such definite and crystal clear functions that there is little danger of misunderstanding, or in boards which are so sharply divided that it is thought best not to take up any fundamental questions lest there be an explosion. There may be wisdom in this more gradual approach; however, there is also danger. Many boards have so indefinitely postponed the task of stating or reviewing objectives that their programs have stagnated, decayed, or died.

27. THE ANNUAL PLAN

One of the best gifts which the chairman of a board or committee can present to his successor is a well-drawn-up annual plan of work. Boards must proceed about their business in some kind of a regular, rhythmical fashion, but it is surprising to discover how many board members fail to realize that fact. They seem to be like the tribe of Indians which was surprised afresh each year by the advent of spring.

An annual plan is easy to make. The time to begin is when a chairman has just been selected. On a sheet of paper marked out by months, he records all the dates which are already established by the constitution, by-laws, or custom, such as the dates of the regular meetings of the board, of the annual meeting, and of the budget hearings. He then puts down his own tentative judgment about all other matters which have a periodic nature. For example, when should the executive committee meet, when should each special committee be appointed, when should it report, when should the annual solicitation for funds begin, when should the benefit be held, when should the budget be brought to the board, when should there be an annual review of objectives, and when should the board report to its constituency? In this first formulation of target dates, the executive can be a great help.

During the year, the chairman should keep this plan of work by him, making periodic notations as to when he finds it most effective to do things. He will almost certainly have to revise his earlier dates and there will be many more that he should add. Gradually, however, there will be built up a kind of master plan or schedule, particularly if the chairman carries on his responsibilities for a subsequent year or years.

When a new chairman is selected, the person who is retiring should review his plan and put it in order so that he can discuss it and turn it over to his successor. The new person in turn, in the light of his own experience, will want to make certain modifications and additions. He will, however, have the great advantage of seeing his whole duties spelled out for the year, with suggested dates for originating matters, for issuing reminders, and for establishing finish lines. The annual plan will become one of the chief tools he can use in being an effective chairman.

The illustration given has been that of the chairman of a board, but the same kind of annual plan can also be worked out by every other officer of the board and every chairman of a standing committee. The concreteness and clarity of the board's work will be greatly enhanced by the routinization of all matters that can be made routine.

28. THE MEETINGS OF THE BOARD[2]

The board members are the most powerful people in the world of the agency or association. When they come together to pool their best judgments, the result should be challenging and exciting. The plain fact of the matter, however, is that all too often it is not. The chief problem with most board meetings is simply that they are not very interesting. One veteran member put the matter rather pungently when she remarked: "Not all board meetings are dull; some of them are cancelled."

Two observations should be made at once. First, people do not join boards to have fun and it is inappropriate to imply that they do. Second, the chief

---

[2] An unusually good discussion of the proper handling of meetings may be found in Roy Sorenson, *The Art of Board Membership* (New York: Association Press, 1950), Chapter V.

function of the board is to solve problems, and problems have a way of being sticky, tedious, complicated, and baffling. But the tedium and apathy which characterize so many board meetings is often a symptom of deeper troubles which cannot be dealt with adequately unless a positive and constructive approach is made to the meetings of the board.

Those meetings are the crucial moments in the continuing life of the board. It is then that policy is made, that lines of direction are laid down, that the group spirit is renewed, and that the individual member gains a fresh enthusiasm. Attendance at meetings is generally thought to be a first requisite of membership on a board, and this opinion is wholly correct; for, after all, a board is essentially a collective enterprise. Widespread absences from meetings or failures to achieve the values that only they can contribute is a sure evidence that corrective measures need to be taken.[3] There are at least six major ways of improving the situation:

First, *the patterns and procedures of board meetings should be reduced to routine as far as possible, so that constant decisions do not need to be made about*

---

[3] Benjamin Franklin is said to have secured a resolution of the board of Pennsylvania Hospital to the effect that "each member is to pay two shillings sixpence for total absence and one shilling for not coming on time and for every hour's absence after the fixed time, sixpence per hour, all of which fines to be disposed of as the majority shall direct. The town clock, or should that not strike, the watch of the oldest person present to be the standard for determining the time." (Sloan, p. 13, *op. cit.* in Bibliography.)

them. Among the matters which can usually be regularized are these: the time, place, and frequency of the regular meetings; the procedure which should be followed in order to call special meetings; the circumstances under which meetings are to be open or closed to outsiders (a special problem for public boards); and such necessary rules of practice as the establishment of a quorum. Boards may not always be able to follow the customs they establish; but to the extent that they can do so, they will save themselves constant and tedious discussions about procedural matters.

The proper development of the agenda is also important, and the following practices define the customary procedure. The agenda should be made by the executive and approved by the chairman of the board. It should be sent out in advance of the meeting to all members so that they will have time to study it and to examine any supporting documents. Except in rare cases, the agenda should not be ironclad but should be subject to revision at the meeting if the members want to revise it. It should always, if possible, allow time for free discussion at the end of the session. The items listed should not be merely sketchy notations indicating generally what is to be discussed but should be stated at such length that the board will know what to expect. The person responsible for the presentation of each item should be clearly indicated.

Second, *the board meeting should be a culmina-*

tion of a long process of preparation. As has already been seen in other connections, a board has a continuing life of its own and the groundwork for most actions should be laid before the time of the meeting itself. Committees should have sifted the evidence and come to the point of recommendations. The person most familiar with a particular problem should have the responsibility for summarizing it for the whole board. In general, the meetings of the board should be only the peaks of a continuing flow of interest and activity in the life of the board.

Third, *reports made to the board should be as well presented as possible.* Much of the time of most meetings is spent reading or listening to reports. Therefore it is important to establish a tradition that wherever possible reports shall be written out and distributed, that they be brief and interesting, and that they highlight the major points which are to be made. The members of a committee should be concerned not only with reaching the proper conclusions but also with communicating them effectively. Sometimes the chairman needs to provide encouragement or help to the individuals concerned to enable them to do their reporting effectively.

Fourth, *as much of the time of the meeting should be reserved for discussion as is possible.* The wisdom of the board results from the pooling of the viewpoints of its members; the best possible decision on any issue usually comes when it has been thoroughly discussed. Moreover, discussion is a form of active

134

participation and therefore creates both involvement and a sense of responsibility on the part of the members. "Discussion" is, to be sure, a term which can be used to cover a multitude of social sins: set speeches following one another without any relationship among them; mere conversation which has no relevance to the point at issue; floundering about without clarifying the issues; participation by a few while the rest remain silent; a series of observations made by the board members as the chairman calls upon them; and all the other ways of seeming to have a discussion without really having one, ways which are familiar to everyone who has ever been in a meeting.

Real discussion, the kind which the board should have, has a far different tone and spirit. There is a focus on the issues and a progression from one point to the next. People participate as they are moved to do so, and their remarks have relationship to one another. The chairman plays an important but not a dominant role in stating and summarizing issues, helping the group to stay on the subject, keeping unobtrusively in command of the situation while still insisting that the conversation shall be general and not always directed toward him, and preventing any of the excesses or perversions of the discussion method mentioned in the last paragraph. There is a simple test as to whether a discussion has been vital or not; if it has been, its participants feel rewarded and stimulated.

Fifth, *there should be as much informality as possible*. Boards with good social relationships among the members are more likely to have good board meetings than those where the members do not know each other well. Board members who are unacquainted with one another feel stiff and dull, reluctant to talk, awkward, and overformal. This situation should be relieved wherever possible by means which have already been described.

Not all boards are so fortunate as to have the integration which makes informality possible. Public boards often feel that they must retain a greater austerity of approach than private boards do. It is worth noting that public boards almost never have their meetings at mealtime, while private boards usually do. This difference is caused in part because public boards usually have open meetings and private boards have closed ones. But on both public and private boards there are other reasons contributing to formalism. If the board has strong factionalism, if its members are not used to working with one another, if feeling on issues runs so high that it transcends the capacity of the group spirit to contain it, then the conduct of the meeting must be formal in order to permit any business at all to be transacted.

Underlying all meetings are certain fundamental rules of parliamentary procedure which are soundly based on logic and precedent. Robert's *Rules of Order* is probably one of the most frequently consulted books in the world. But a board should not be too rigorous in its use of parliamentary practice; there is no better way to tie itself up almost endlessly in routines and procedures. The best way to operate is to discuss a matter until there appears to be consensus. Then, for the sake of the record, a motion can be formulated which seems to embody the viewpoint of everyone. Since consensus is not always possible, there must occasionally be recourse to more formal procedures, but consensus is more desirable.

Sixth, *meetings should be kept brief.* This point is so important as to deserve separate mention but so obvious as to need no discussion!

The responsibility for making meetings effective in these six ways falls heavily on the chairman of the board and the executive, particularly the former. The role of the chairman is not easy to describe since it varies with the situation as well as with the personality of the man or woman concerned. Certainly, however, the chairman should be well versed in all the matters scheduled on the agenda. He should be clearly in control of the meeting. During the course of it, he should do whatever seems to be comfortable or right in the immediate situation. He must be sure that all viewpoints are expressed, even drawing them out of silent members if that proves necessary. During the discussion, he should err on the side of being silent rather than on the side of talking too much. In presenting the situation or the problem originally, he will often have had an opportunity to indicate his own feeling; indeed it is hard for him not to do so. Therefore he must be sure that other people are equally free to express their own views. He must realize too that when the members of a board participate in a discussion, they are becoming involved, and increased involvement brings increased interest. Throughout the meeting, he must keep in his mind the necessity of coming to the best possible decision on the issue involved. If he can, however, he should see that any decision is arrived at in the right way— on the basis of all known facts and after the fullest and freest participation possible.

The executive should be present at all meetings of the board except at those times in which it is discussing his own employment or salary or successor. Most boards make provision on the agenda for a report by the executive, and this is his major opportunity to state his views. Aside from that, however, he should play only a minor part in the actual conduct of the meeting. Though he does not need to impose a vow of silence on himself, and indeed should speak up on any matter on which he feels strongly or believes that he has special knowledge not possessed by the board, he is usually wise to leave most of the actual participation to the members themselves. Certainly he should not aim at being a successful politician with supporters on the board. Rather he is a reporter, presenting not only his own opinions but all other facts necessary for the board to reach a judgment.

29. GETTING BOARD MEMBERS TO ACCEPT RESPONSIBILITY

The failure of a board member to accept responsibility is a sign that the board is not operating efficiently. The member concerned was not well chosen, he was not inducted properly, he does not know what his specific responsibilities are, he does not really understand the objectives of the program, he finds the meetings dull: these and other reasons contribute to his inaction. The correction of such conditions is the best *general* way of increasing the participation of board members. But most boards have at least a few members who do not take on so large a share of the responsibility as they should and they constitute a *special* problem and challenge, particularly for the chairman and the executive.

The distinction between *general* and *special* is the crux of the matter. It is seldom possible to get a whole group of people interested and active all at the same time. Some board chairmen hope that this principle is not true and that there is some device which will change the pattern of behavior of a board. Other chairmen believe that they can accomplish the same end by lecturing the board about its duty, a method which almost always has an effect precisely opposite from that intended. People participate best when they are interested or challenged, not when they are made to feel guilty. In order to get people to accept responsibility, therefore, it is first necessary to arouse their interest. Now the first (and perhaps the only) principle of creating interest is this: *the new interest must be attached to an existing interest.* Since the interest pattern of each individual is unique, it follows that if people are to be persuaded to take responsibility, they must be dealt with individually.

The skillful board chairman does this all the time. He knows that Mr. A is concerned with the program, though he has been passive; he will respond best to a frank and open request for help. Mrs. B, because of an event in her personal life, has a deep interest in one part of the program; he tries therefore to see that her board assignments relate to that part but also that she comes in contact with other aspects of the work so that her outlook is broadened. Mr. C likes Mr. D; therefore the chairman knows that if he asks Mr. C to participate with Mr. D in some project, he is more likely to get active work. Mrs. E is interested in gaining more status in a particular circle in the community and would be happy to accept an assignment which is likely to bring her closer to this goal. Mr. F likes challenges; if it is suggested that he *might* be able to do something which other board members might not be capable of handling, he may rise to the occasion.

As these examples suggest, the best way to get an apathetic board member to take responsibility is to persuade him to accept an assignment—one which is congenial to him, which really needs to be done, which he can accomplish readily, and for which he can receive some recognition of his efforts. This first task should then be followed by another. It will usually be a long time before a chairman can change a thoroughly apathetic member into one who is deeply involved in the board's activities. Usually, however, the only way to achieve this result is by the route of gradualism.

If a board has a large number of apathetic people, the chairman should review the membership to try to find those key individuals on whom to concentrate his effort. On any board, there are usually a few people who have marked influence on the other members. If these leaders can be persuaded to accept responsibility, their own resulting support and interest will prove to be contagious.

The executive also has an important part to play in increasing the participation of board members. His first duty is to counsel with and to support the chairman. The executive often has ideas or insights about the nature of the board members' present interests which are useful in helping to work out a pattern of assignments. Also he can try to support and reinforce any line of strategy which the chairman may be following; in the case of Mrs. B, for example, the executive can often suggest ways by which she can help the part of the program in which she is most deeply interested.

The executive may also do a great deal directly to get board members to accept responsibility, being sure that he is acting in accord with the wishes of the chairman. The executive's best method of operation is to ask an apathetic board member for counsel and advice. Everybody likes to be consulted, and the board member will probably be flattered if he is asked for help; but only if the executive has a real problem and the member can give real help. Executives can do other things as well: provide special information to a board member in terms of some known interest he possesses in the program; arrange for him to attend meetings or undertake tours of inspection which deal with the program; and be sure that his special accomplishments are recognized.

But everything which the chairman, the executive, or anyone else can do will finally go back to two fundamental ideas: People are always interested specifically, not generally. And a new interest must be created by attaching it to a present one.

30. THE BOARD AND ITS PUBLICS

By its very nature, the board is the central instrument for interpreting the program to those people outside it whose support is essential or desirable. A board member is usually chosen because he represents some facet of the community or constituency. This fact puts him at once into the position of explaining and supporting the program to those whom he represents. Sometimes he does this interpretation formally, as when a labor representative on a board reports back to his own union. Much more frequently, the reporting is informal. It occurs as the

142

member uses his personal contacts and associations to help people understand the work of the agency or association on whose board he sits.

Sometimes bad public relations occur simply because the board is not sufficiently representative of the important groups which should be consulted. For example, a private home for unwed mothers was located in a prosperous suburb, but none of the board members of the institution lived in the community. The home was unpopular with its neighbors; it was, in fact, almost in a state of siege, with bad consequences for everyone concerned. When it was decided to confront the issue directly and some of the leaders of the community were persuaded to join the board, the tensions began to disappear.

This illustration suggests the important fact that every board must deal with many special publics. A useful way to begin thinking about community relationships is, in fact, to analyze the major groups which need to be influenced. Consider, for example, a church-supported liberal arts college. Its board must realize that its publics include the alumni, the students, their parents, the members of the religious denomination, the people who live near the college, the donors of funds, the various public and private regulatory agencies who have some authority over the college, the association of colleges to which this one belongs, and so on. Each agency or association has its own distinctive list of such publics as these. The value in spelling out the categories of influence

143

and relationship in this way is that it gives insights into special approaches as well as some idea of what groups may be overlooked. The board of the college, for example, after making the above list, might conclude that it was not doing enough to interpret the program to the alumni and to the members of the denomination. The identification of these groups would provide a focus for further public relations efforts.

The special publics with which a board may wish to be concerned are not all defined by its own relationships with them. A community has many special groupings of people and one method of approach to the community is to work through them. This point has been very well put in a volume dealing with school boards:

> The total population served by a board member is divided into many publics. Some may consist of groups comparable economically and inclined to think, vote, and act somewhat alike. Other groups may represent a diversity of conditions, including geographic locations, sex, age, occupation, profession, and civic organization. Still others may be drawn together by common interests; by emergencies, real or imaginary; or by the capricious vagaries of common gossip. All together they will include the chamber of commerce, labor groups, taxpayers associations, ministerial associations, parent-teacher associations, neighborhood groups, veterans organizations, women's clubs, luncheon clubs, fraternal groups,

144

church groups, and a hundred and one other varieties; yet not one of them could be said to represent the mythical "general public." Each group has its own peculiar interests in education and its own designs for their promotion.[4]

This emphasis on the special publics of an agency or association does not rule out the possibility of reaching many or all of them by the same means. A feature story about the program in a newspaper or a magazine or a special television show built around some activity will come to the attention of very large numbers of people. But though someone may be impressed by the recognition accorded to the program, his sense of identification with it will have been built up around his own special relationship. He will interpret the story in terms of that relationship. The account of the opening of a new clinic in a private hospital, for example, will be received differently by the donors of the funds, the constituency, the staff and board members of other hospitals, and the potential patients in the clinic.

Because of the importance of the board's community responsibility, it should pay particular attention to the public relations activities of the agency or association. This work must go forward under the direction of the executive, but the board needs to give it special guidance and assistance. Since the members are

---

[4] *School Boards in Action,* 24th Yearbook of the American Association of School Administrators. Washington, D. C., 1946, pp. 197-198.

145

themselves a part of the larger community outside the agency or association, they can speak with authority on such matters as the effectiveness of promotional materials or annual reports, the best approaches to the newspapers, the television stations or other mass media, and the subtle patterns of influence which cause a program to be accepted or rejected in important sections of the community.

Many aspects of the board's responsibility have important public relations consequences. Indeed it might well be claimed that everything about an agency or association is somehow related to its effect on the community. Even the best kind of public relations cannot make a program look very much better than it really is—at least for very long. We have it on high authority that "you cannot fool all of the people all of the time." Perhaps the most important thing a board can do, however, in assuring effective community contacts is to have an excellent executive and staff. To most people the employed staff represents the program, both while its members are at work and in their own private lives. People think about a university in terms of its professors and about a hospital in terms of its medical and nursing staff. A board, therefore, must realize that in all matters that have to do with personnel, it is dealing with an important aspect of public relations.

An agency which operates in a professional field has a special obligation to it. Conferences, exchange of ideas and techniques, the carrying out of research,

146

the writing of papers for journals: all these are in the nature of good relations with the professional group with which the agency is connected. The board should encourage the executive and staff to participate in such activities as far as possible. Professional leadership is very important to an agency.

One special public relations problem which every board must face is that of external complaint and criticism. Board members may as well remember that people always seem to have opinions about everything, however well- or ill-informed they may be, and that any vital program is going to have those who disagree with all or part of its effort. Ibsen is said to have observed, "When you go out to fight for truth and justice, never wear your best pants," and it is pointless for board members to believe that they can always wear theirs. Not all criticism, to be sure, has to do with general policy. Very often it deals with alleged unwise decisions or with poor administration.

The most frequent form of criticism is that expressed informally in conversations or at social occasions. If a board member is present when a negative comment is made, he should take as constructive an attitude as possible toward it. One good procedure is to ask the critic to amplify his comments and give his evidence; often the result exposes the shallowness of the censure. (The dark and ominous comment, "I could tell you plenty about that agency," may resolve itself into the fact that some of the members of an auxiliary board are not very active!) **If** the expansion of the observations reveals that there is indeed some ground for complaint, the board member should deal with the matter directly. If he knows the answer, he should give it. If not, he should be careful to understand the criticism, getting at all the facts which lie behind it. He should then bring the matter to the attention of the chairman or the executive, asking that it be looked into and a report made back to him. Finally, he should see that the person who made the criticism is informed as to the facts of the case and what, if anything, has been done about it. Such an attitude on his part is the best kind of public relations, for it indicates very tangibly to everyone that he is concerned with the program and has put his own weight behind it.

Another major form of complaint is that which is brought to the board by a hostile delegation. Such an occurrence is more frequent, perhaps, with public boards than with private ones. Such a group may be dealt with by the chairman, by a committee, or by a whole board. Whoever serves in this capacity should hear the delegation out and, in as reasonable a manner as possible, state the agency's side of the case. Sometimes the board is led to modify its own position, sometimes the outside group is mollified by a fuller understanding of the situation, and sometimes the discussion results in stalemate. Whatever the outcome, openness of approach is usually the best policy. Even a group which goes away angry at a decision cannot be quite so angry as before with the board which made it.

The third major form of criticism is that brought about by the open enmity of some individual or group directed against the board itself. A mayor or a governor may come into conflict with a public board which he cannot control, a newspaper may launch an attack, or some group with profoundly opposing views to those expressed in the program may try to wrest control away from the present board. In such cases, a board may decide to compromise or to submit entirely. If it does not, it is in for a fight, whether it wishes one or not, and it had better do those things which are useful in war: consolidate its position, increase its armament, enlarge the number of its allies, and, if necessary, seize the initiative in the battle.

So far as possible, to be sure, battles should be prevented, not sought. But it is undeniably true that some boards have been set up to protect a certain function of government from partisan politics, and this fact in itself may build a certain amount of tension into the situation. If possible, the board should work closely with the political officials (who, it should be remembered, are also representative public servants) while still retaining its own essential identity. It is necessary to walk the line (often a narrow one) between getting too far away from politics and thereby removing the board from public responsiveness and getting so closely involved in politics that the board loses its own independence.

In the public field, each board tends to have a monopoly of the services which it provides to its community. There is usually only one school board or board of health. Among private agencies, this fact is much less true. Frequently there is a whole cluster of agencies, each with its board, performing the same general type of service. When this is the case the need for co-ordination of agencies—and of their boards—becomes immediately evident, for if duplication or gaps in service are to be avoided, there must be some joint planning of operations.

In the private welfare field, where the need is perhaps the greatest, most has been done to provide means for joint effort. Most large communities now have welfare councils, through which the various boards agree on their respective areas of service. Often, too, there is a co-ordination of fund raising by the various boards, whether through a community fund drive or by other means. Similar kinds of co-ordination also exist in other fields of work; health, religious, and educational agencies and associations are particularly notable in this respect.

Public agencies of various sorts do have an obligation to work together for their common purposes. Thus a state board of education, a state board of regents of institutions of higher learning, and a state library board have certain common responsibilities. Some co-ordination is provided by the fact that all three agencies are part of the structure of state government, but this integration is often more apparent

150

than real. Occasionally, these various kinds of public boards develop a common program, as when all of them make a united budget request to the legislature. Also, provisions are sometimes made for overlapping memberships or the *ex officio* representation on the boards of certain public officials.

In both private and public fields, boards which have entered into agreements must abide by them. Usually a large share of the burden of collaboration falls on the executive. It is he who must implement the board's policies and it is he who must work closely with the executives of the other agencies. An ambitious executive may sometimes find it difficult to keep within the limits imposed by a joint program of service; if so, his board must help him to see the value of a common effort. Boards sometimes grow ambitious too and want to go beyond the area of service to which they have agreed; in such a case, it is the executive who must point out the limitations by which the agency is bound.

Still another situation exists when there are hierarchies of boards. In a large city, for example, there may be a number of autonomous neighborhood YMCA's each with its own board but with a central board co-ordinating the work of all of them. Also national associations with their own boards often have local chapters with boards. The hierarchy is made possible and can work effectively only if there is a careful allocation of responsibilities to each level. Another important factor which eases such collaboration is the respect which the lower boards have for the higher, a respect which is often based on the prestige of the members of the latter. Usually these members have had experience on the lower boards and, because of the excellence of their abilities and their general prestige in the community, have earned their place on the higher board.

Reference has already been made to associations of boards and board members in terms of their value as educational instruments. Such associations also have an important function in helping to secure understanding and support for the field of work concerned. Such associations can represent their member boards in seeking desirable legislation and in representation before various governmental agencies. They can study the problems of co-ordination with other agencies providing related services. They can provide national and regional planning on the work of the field with which they are connected.

This rather long section has dealt with many aspects of the public relations responsibilities of the board. The importance of the problem must be understood, however, for no agency or association can live unto itself. It is the responsibility of every board member, inherent in his very selection, that he shall be a bridge to the community doing whatever he can to extend the public understanding of the program. To paraphrase an ancient observation, a board that wakes up to find itself famous hasn't been asleep.

31. MEASURING THE SUCCESS OF THE PROGRAM

Boards need to know how well the program is succeeding. The support and effort they give should have some results. If the work is effective, that fact is good to know, for everybody likes to be part of a successful enterprise. The only danger in such a case is complacency, for, as an old folk saying has it, "The good is the enemy of the best." If the program is not going well, the board certainly needs to know that too, so that it can take the proper corrective measures.

The work of reporting on the program, including some assessment of successes or failures, must be that of the executive and staff. They alone have the facts on which judgment must be based. But it is essential to realize that evaluation is always a dual, interacting process of getting facts and seeing what they mean. For example, a private day care center may have a decline in the number of different nursery school children participating. This fact taken alone looks ominous, but when the executive explains that it is a result of the staff's effort to persuade parents to keep their children in the school, a wholly different light is cast on the situation, particularly when the statistics show that the average length of stay per child has increased.

The board can help the executive to appraise the facts and determine their meaning. The practical outlook of the board, as well as its fresh, nonspecialist approach, are usually helpful in arriving at a more

153

exact and easily understood evaluation. Also the diverse viewpoints of the members make it possible for them to look at the data from many different angles. The executive who goes through a periodic evaluation session with his board will find that he can do a progressively better job as his own insight deepens.

Success can be measured in only one way: how well were the objectives achieved? The approach is somewhat different, however, depending on whether the measurement has to do with specific or with general objectives.

The board which has set up specific objectives for a given period of time should, at the end of that time, measure its success in achieving them. The museum which wants in one year to add a major acquisition, to sponsor three special displays, to add a full-time research worker, and to increase the number of students in the museum school must ask itself at the end of the year whether it reached all these goals. On the answer to that question depends not only the judgment as to past success but some estimate as to future progress. If the board has exceeded its expectations, goals can be set higher for next year. If it has failed, it must ask itself why, and what meaning that failure has for the board's own activities. Should the same goal be set for another year with the implication that the board must intensify its efforts? Or should a lower goal be set?

The measurement of success in achieving general objectives differs in various kinds of programs. In almost every field of work, there are well-developed methods of collecting evidence. Schools have achievement tests, libraries have circulation figures, hospitals and other kinds of institutions have rating scales, and colleges have accrediting procedures. The following list of some major kinds of evidence on which a board may base its judgment is therefore merely illustrative.

In a number of programs, the method of evaluation is inherent in the very nature of the enterprise. The clearest example is to be found in private industry where success is measured by the making of a profit. Another illustration might be that of a vocational rehabilitation agency, where success would be determined by the number of disabled people placed in a work situation who adjust to it.

The most frequent method of evaluation is probably the counting of the number of people who participate or the extent of the use of the services provided. The number of books taken from a library, the number of people who attend an evening school, the number of people who are treated in a hospital, and the number of mothers who come to a well-baby clinic are all examples of this sort of reporting. Such statistics on the extent of use may be either gross or refined; the librarian, for example, may merely count the total number of books circulated or may make a much more detailed analysis on the basis of the subject matter of the books which are issued. The counting of numbers also gains significance when figures are compared with those in other similar situations. The library board may be much interested in seeing how its per capita circulation compares with that of another city. One warning must always be issued concerning measures of the extent of service: they are not qualitative. One may know the number of books circulated and still not know whether they were read, or whether they had any effect on the readers, or whether, if so, that effect was desirable.

An allied kind of evaluation is that which occurs through an examination of community statistics. Departments of health look closely at the disease and death rates in their communities to determine the effect of various campaigns. A concerted and continued effort to prevent a certain kind of illness may have pronounced effects. This same kind of evidence is also used by a number of other governmental agencies, particularly in welfare and education.

Some agencies make efforts to collect the opinions of those who use their services or of the general public. Market research to appraise the consumers' reactions to a product is a standard practice in private industry, as is the careful analysis of complaints. In any situation in which the measurement of public opinion is used, board members should realize that it is now a job for an expert. The board will have its own ideas about the reactions of people to whom board members have talked, but such contacts may be unrepresentative of the total population concerned.

Sometimes the only kind of evidence which may be secured is that which comes from case studies or the reporting of important incidents. In both, it is assumed that the situation chosen is somehow indicative of the whole. Even though this assumption may be questioned, it is often useful to have as much evidence as the case or the incident can provide. For example, the intensive analysis of a number of cases handled by a family service agency may be revealing. To a settlement house operating in an area of marked racial tension, any incidents which show successful integration may also seem significant.

One final form of evaluation which may be worthy of mention is the outside appraisal which is made by some expert or group of experts in the field. Occasionally these appraisals are regular and systematic; for example, the accrediting procedures used in colleges and universities normally call for periodic visitation of the institution to inspect its work. In most situations, however, outside surveys or appraisals are called for only under special circumstances. In the normal course of operations, it is essential that the executive support the idea of such an inspection; indeed, it is best if the recommendation originates with the executive.

In measuring the success of any program, no one kind of evidence is adequate. The board needs to be certain that it secures all the data relevant to the situation. There is always a limit to the amount of time an executive, a staff, and a board can spend on ap-

157

praisal. Exact and detailed research evaluations are not usually possible in the flow of work of a busy agency or association. But, within the realm of practicality, as much evaluation should be carried out as is possible. The board will find such activity richly rewarding.

32. BOARDS WITH SERIOUS DIFFICULTIES

Throughout this book, it has been stressed that a board can get into all kinds of difficulties with respect to its own internal situation, its relationships within the agency or association, or its interaction with its constituency or its publics. But it is normal for a board to have problems; if there were none, why have a board? Then, too, some difficulties which look like problems really are conditions of life; most agencies and associations, for example, never have enough money to do everything they would like to do. In such situations, one is reminded of the man who had a heavy crop of dandelions in his lawn. After trying every method he could discover to get rid of them, he finally wrote to the state college of agriculture listing all his efforts and asking, "What shall I do now?" Before very long, the reply came back, "We suggest you learn to love them." Boards may not grow to love their difficulties; but often they might as well get used to them.

The central thesis of this book is, of course, that most of the problems of boards can be solved, at least partially, by informed and persistent effort. The

158

difficulties of boards are so numerous and varied as to defy description, but some of the major ones are inertia, a narrow social perspective, dominance by undue political influence, violent internal or external conflict, senility, factionalism, incapacity to work with the executive and staff, domination by a member or group of members, members who use the board to pursue special interests of their own, subservience to the executive, and nepotism.

Ways to cure all these illnesses, and many more besides, have been suggested elsewhere in this book in connection with the various principles and practices suggested. Once such problems have emerged, they can usually be dealt with only in terms of the use of such principles and practices, although the remedy may take a long time to apply. Naturally it is best if the board is structured and operated so well that the problems never have a real chance to emerge.

But boards are not always so wise and therefore they may deteriorate, sometimes very badly. The responsibility of every board member requires that he sense as best he can the approach of damaging situations and do everything in his power to avert them. It is often an unpleasant task to deal with them and therefore too frequently they are allowed to grow worse because nobody has the courage to face them. Sometimes a member finally feels that he must resign but he should do so only as a last resort, for his greatest services lie in standing up to the problem and helping to combat it.

The chairman has the major responsibility for the effectiveness of the board, but it is a responsibility which is shared by every member. Whoever feels that a situation is getting out of hand might well proceed by asking himself three questions:

The first is, "Am I myself the problem?" To ask this question and to try to give as honest and objective an answer as possible may well provide a serious shock to the chairman or the member who asks it of himself, for he may suddenly realize that it is he himself or his own actions that create the difficulty. He had always felt that the board needed continuity of leadership; could it really be that his own lengthy tenure as chairman has created stagnation? Could one's own firmness have been interpreted by others as stubbornness, could the special emphasis on one part of the program look like failure to be responsible for the whole, and could an effort to safeguard the board against the machinations of others look like either possessiveness or factionalism? Such questions are never comfortable but they need to be asked, particularly by anyone who is setting himself up to be the purifier of the board.

If the answer to the first question is "yes," the chairman or member should take such steps as seem appropriate. If it is "no," a second major question should be asked: "Can the board solve the problem itself?" Once again a question of judgment is raised. If the board has within itself the capacity to remedy the difficulty it should certainly do so, for such a process will strengthen its own capacity to deal with other situations and may well bring to the board the self-confidence which it needs.

But if the answer is once again "no," then a third question must be asked: "Whom can we get to help us out of the difficulty?" In case of illness, one calls the doctor. Sometimes this principle is as useful for a board as for an individual, even though the knowledge of the specialist on boards is neither so exact nor so comprehensive as that of a physician. Still there are a great many experienced people who might be brought into the situation and who can both diagnose the difficulties and suggest remedies. A welfare agency might turn to its own council of social agencies. A hospital might consult the American Hospital Association. A library might try to get the help of its state library agency or the American Library Association. A school might seek the advice of the state department of education or the state or national school board association. University professors in the relevant disciplines may be brought in, and so may outstanding chairmen of the boards of other similar agencies. Any such person or group, however, can only make suggestions on which the board itself can act. The doctor is a diagnostician, not a surgeon.

All the foregoing remarks have implied that boards must correct their own serious problems. Fortunately, however, there is another source of improvement: the outside authority which supports or appoints the

161

board. If things get too bad, the constituency may elect a new board, either through the usual processes or by means of a recall of present members so that there is a clean sweep. A mayor or a governor may likewise move as rapidly as possible to change the board through the power of appointment. Since such changes are usually unpleasant and filled with tension and the new board may be completely unprepared for its heavy new responsibilities, it is certainly best if the normal processes of board improvement are carried out from within. But it is fortunate for society that if boards do not solve their own difficulties, there are often outside authorities who will eventually step in.

To bring matters to their logical conclusion, it may as well be pointed out that boards can die. Sometimes they, and their agencies or associations, disappear because they have outlived their time; their purpose no longer justifies their existence in the modern world. Sometimes they die because they have become too sick and stubborn to get well. They have turned in upon themselves, refused to call the doctor, and moved toward sudden or lingering death.

Sometimes, though, boards go out of existence with their flags flying. A board may honestly believe that its work has been done. Or, as in the case of several neighboring school districts which consolidate into one, several boards may be succeeded by a single one. Such cases as these are victories, not defeats, for they demonstrate an awareness of new or larger values.

CHAPTER SIX

33. The Success of the Board

A GOOD board is a victory, not a gift. The central idea of this book is that in this area of our social life excellence cannot be achieved without informed thought and constant effort, usually expended over a long period of time. Sometimes outstanding boards seem not to have any problems; they operate so smoothly and efficiently and well that they make everything appear easy. But this is an outside view and it is not to be trusted.

Superlative performance in any aspect of life always looks far more simple than it is. The expert figure skater sweeps swiftly across the ice, gliding, turning, pirouetting, and leaping, with never a lost motion and with an incomparably graceful ease. It almost seems that anybody could do the same. Anyone who has ever been on a pair of skates, however, knows how false that idea is. He realizes that it took countless hours of practice to achieve the simplicity of perfection. So it is with boards. The effective ones

163

have achieved their positions not by accident but by design—and by a great deal of hard labor carried out over a long time.

But though boards are long-range enterprises, they also operate in cycles. Theirs is not a constant steady sweep forward but a rhythm which is attuned to the program or the budget or the tenure of the chairman. There are recurrent times when boards pause to take stock, to make plans for the coming period, and to put special board responsibilities into new hands. At such a time it is appropriate to appraise the success of the board.

The ultimate test is the success of the program. There is really not very much point in having a board if the purpose of the agency or association is not achieved. To be sure the success might be in spite of the board or without any very great contribution from it, but ordinarily good boards are associated with good programs.

Aside from having a good program, the best test of a board is the extent to which it conforms to the sound principles of good board practice. If the reader is on a board, he has probably paused again and again throughout this book to evaluate that board in terms of the standards or procedures suggested. This kind of comparison is probably the only valid way by which success—or failure—can be appraised. Several examples may make this point more concrete.

A major instrument of appraisal is the rating scale in the Appendix. As the reader will perceive, this

164

scale is a composite which takes into account certain major points which are most useful in evaluating all aspects of a board. This rating scale may be used as a device by means of which the chairman, or the executive committee, or a special group, or even the whole board can score the board periodically. Presumably, if the resulting profile is not a perfectly vertical line at the far left, the need for progress will be indicated. If it is, the direction of future development should be clear. Periodic profiles kept over the years provide a record of board growth and a guide to future administrations.

If a board chooses, it may use a number of the special sections of this book as means of setting up rating scales of its own. For example, a board which wished to concentrate on its proper functions would find it fairly easy to work out another rating scale, using the sixteen items suggested in Chapter Four, perhaps adding or subtracting from that list in terms of the board's own judgment of what is appropriate.

Some segment of the board's work may also provide the focus for the development of a special instrument. One such was suggested in Chapter Two in the chart developed to analyze the nature of the board of the "Home for Destitute University Professors." Probably the items suggested there are too simple for most situations, but the form itself may be expanded to include the criteria to be used.

The ultimate purpose of making an appraisal of any sort is not to discover how well the board has done but to give it an opportunity to know how to improve itself. One looks back in order to look forward to see what changes need to be made—and then to make them. Thus, operating in cycles and going through recurrent procedures but always at higher levels, the board improves itself. It moves not in a circle but in an upward spiral.

In the first chapter it was pointed out that to become properly aware of the real nature of familiar objects and influences, it is necessary to bring them squarely into view, examining them with the same wonder and curiosity with which one would inspect the rare or the previously unknown. That familiar phenomenon, the board, has been subjected to such a view in this book with the result that viewed in its large perspective, it is seen to be a complex, difficult, but fascinating part of American life, with a great present and future significance. To paraphrase Henry Adams, a board affects eternity; it can never tell where its influence stops.

Board activity is one of the many ways by which human beings spend their life energies. It is more than a mere outlet: it is a generator as well. Vitality in boards comes from the planning which helps to channel men's efforts; from the sense of accomplishment which rewards well-directed power; and from meaningful activity where hitherto untapped reserves of strength are released by the challenge of a larger than personal goal.

Boards are human and complex because they have

inherited the characteristics of their creators who are complex human beings. They are the products of creative people who have found a way of extending their thought and action beyond their own mortal span. They continue to challenge the best that is in mankind to use them effectively in the management of socially significant human affairs.

34. Bibliography

American Association of School Administrators. *School Boards in Action.* Washington: American Association of School Administrators, 1946.

Bemis, Maynard, and others. *Boardsmanship, a Guide for the School Board Member.* Stanford: Stanford University Press, 1955.

Brown, Courtney C., and Smith, E. Everett, eds. *The Director Looks at His Job.* New York: Columbia University Press, 1957.

Copeland, Melvin T., and Towl, Andrew R. *Board of Directors and Business Management.* Cambridge: Harvard Business School, 1947.

Garceau, Oliver. *Public Library in the Political Process.* New York: Columbia University Press, 1949.

Hall, Anna Gertrude. *The Library Trustee.* Chicago: American Library Association, 1937.

Letourneau, Charles V. *Hospital Trusteeship.* Chicago: Starling Publications, 1959.

Manley, Marian Catherine. *A Handbook for Library Trustees.* New York: R. R. Bowker Company, 1959.

Routzahn, Mary Swain. *Better Board Meetings*. New York: National Publicity Council for Health and Welfare Services, 1952.

Sloan, Raymond P. *This Hospital Business of Ours*. New York: Putnam, 1952.

Sorenson, Roy. *The Art of Board Membership*. New York: Association Press, 1950.

————. *How to Be a Board or Committee Member*. New York: Association Press, 1954.

Tuttle, Edward M. *School Board Leadership in America*. Chicago: Interstate, 1958.

A Rating Scale for Boards

THE CHART for "A Rating Scale for Boards" on page 172 was developed by asking a large number of experienced board members what they considered to be the characteristics of a good board. The list of answers was a long one, reflecting many different points of view, but, as finally refined and reworded, the twelve characteristics shown on the rating scale received virtually unanimous agreement.

This book will be most useful if the reader actually rates a board which he knows well. The way to do this is to think about each characteristic as it applies to that board and then make a choice as to how the board ranks on the five-point scale suggested. This judgment will not be easy to make, but the process of thinking is more valuable than the specific spot where the X is placed. After the board has been rated on each characteristic, a line should be drawn from one mark to another. The result will be a profile of the board.

This profile will show in what ways the board needs to be improved. Ideally a straight line should connect all the dots in the "excellent" column. Insofar as any rating falls farther to the right than that, the board has room for improvement.

At the end of this Appendix, the board characteristics are repeated and are keyed to the numbered sections of the book in which suggestions for solving various problems are presented. To know how to strengthen the board at given points, one should consult the relevant sections. They will provide ideas as to how the board may be improved in specific ways. Later on it will be useful to draw a new profile. The difference between the old and the new will then indicate progress—or the lack of it.

It is appropriate to ask who should do the rating suggested. The best and briefest answer to that question is, "Anyone who wants to do so!" But certain people may be particularly concerned, such as any of the following persons or groups:

1. The chairman of a board who feels a responsibility for improving it during his term of office.

2. The executive committee, the nominating committee, or any other group whose responsibility requires its members to examine the board as a whole.

3. Any board member who wants to work toward improving the present situation.

4. A new board member who wants to learn how to be effective and who performs the rating with the idea of improving his own understanding.

171

A RATING SCALE FOR BOARDS

Characteristics	Excellent	How the Board Rates Good	Average	Poor	Very Poor
A. The board should be made up of effective individuals who can supplement one another's talents.					
B. The board should represent the interests which are to be consulted in formulating policy.					
C. The board should be large enough to carry all necessary responsibilities but small enough to act as a deliberative group.					
D. The basic structural pattern (board, board officials, committees, executive, and staff) should be clear.					
E. There should be an effective working relationship between the board and the executive and staff.					
F. The members of the board should understand the objectives of the agency or association and how those objectives are achieved by the activities undertaken.					
G. The board should have a feeling of social ease and rapport.					
H. Each member of the board should feel involved and interested in its work.					
I. The board should formulate specific goals to guide its work.					
J. Decisions on policy should be made only after full consideration by all parties concerned with the decision.					
K. The board should be certain that effective community relationships are maintained.					
L. The board should have a sense of progress and accomplishment.					

172

5. An executive who wants to advise and assist his board. He should be careful, however, that in giving this advice and assistance, he does not usurp the authority of the chairman.

6. An appointing or nominating authority—such as a governor, a mayor, or a slate-making committee—which is outside the board itself but feels some responsibility for it.

The reader of whatever sort should be warned that the characteristics and suggestions presented here and later are drawn from general experience and always apply in special ways to each particular situation. Nothing is automatic where boards are concerned. The essence of board membership is the making of judgments.

KEY TO NUMBERED SECTIONS OF THE BOOK

A. *The board should be made up of effective individuals who can supplement one another's talents.* See Sections 1, 2, 3, 4, 5, 6, 7, 12, 13, 16, 25, 32, 34.

B. *The board should represent the interests which are to be consulted in formulating policy.* See Sections 2, 3, 7, 11, 12, 13, 14, 16, 30, 32, 34.

C. *The board should be large enough to carry all necessary responsibilities but small enough to act as a deliberative group.* See Sections 2, 3, 7, 11, 12, 13, 14, 16, 25, 28, 32, 34.

D. *The basic structural pattern (board, board officials, committees, executive, and staff) should be clear.* See Sections 4, 5, 6, 8, 9, 10, 15, 16, 17, 18, 19, 20, 21, 22, 23, 24, 25, 27, 28, 32, 34.

E. *There should be an effective working relationship*

173

between the board and the executive and staff. See Sections 2, 4, 5, 6, 8, 10, 15, 16, 18, 19, 20, 21, 22, 23, 24, 25, 27, 28, 29, 32, 34.

F. *The members of the board should understand the objectives of the agency or association and how those objectives are achieved by the activities undertaken.* See Sections 1, 4, 5, 6, 7, 10, 16, 20, 24, 26, 27, 28, 31, 32, 33, 34.

G. *The board should have a feeling of social ease and rapport.* See Sections 1, 2, 4, 5, 7, 9, 10, 11, 12, 16, 25, 28, 29, 32, 34.

H. *Each member of the board should feel involved and interested in its work.* See Sections 1, 4, 5, 6, 7, 11, 12, 13, 14, 16, 21, 25, 28, 29, 30, 31, 32, 34.

I. *The board should formulate specific goals to guide its work.* See Sections 26, 27, 31, 32, 33, 34.

J. *Decisions on policy should be made only after full consideration by all parties concerned with the decision.* See Sections 2, 5, 7, 9, 11, 16, 20, 25, 26, 28, 32, 34.

K. *The board should be certain that effective community relationships are maintained.* See Sections 2, 3, 4, 6, 7, 10, 11, 12, 13, 16, 17, 27, 30, 32, 34.

L. *The board should have a sense of progress and accomplishment.* See Sections 1, 5, 6, 7, 9, 10, 12, 16, 20, 21, 25, 26, 27, 28, 29, 31, 32, 33, 34.

174